THE MIND POWER SYSTEM

Success Through Mental Strength and Positive Thinking

How to Build an Unshakable Winning Mindset in 6 Steps

by

Patrick Drechsler

Table of Contents

Introduction

Your supervisor at work criticizes you. He doesn't like the draft you submitted. What's more, you handed it in not a day before the due date. "Timed pretty tight, huh?" he provokes with a mischievous grin on his face. You know he has something against you. *It doesn't matter when you turn in the draft, as long as it's on time!* But he just has to say something anyway. Or maybe he's right? After all, you never managed to take criticism well, always letting it affect you personally. By the end of this harsh workday, through your entire evening off, and into the next few days, you are seething inside; you feel insecure, and you don't feel like working – all because of some criticism from a superior who doesn't like you.

Exhausting superiors and a lack of critical faculties are only a couple of the many difficulties that people tend to suffer from. Have you ever experienced wanting something badly enough, but you just lacked the discipline to achieve it? You kept putting off that thing that was so close to your heart until eventually, your dream fizzled out? Instead, you stayed on your hamster wheel and there you remain, hoping that this book will give you the consistency to realize your dreams in the future. I'm here to tell you that *it will*.

This book will show you the right way to deal with those superiors who have it in for you, through the cultivation of *mental strength*. Being mentally strong means being resilient. Resilient to deal with losses such as financial hardships or the death of a loved one. That doesn't mean that you can't cry and grieve. But it *does mean* that you won't lose your motivation, zest for life and confidence because of it.

In all of our lives, we face challenges that require us to embody mental strength in many different ways – challenges are unavoidable. But what we can change, is our ability to deal with them effectively.

This book will show you how to deal with all of the challenges that life can throw at you. It will show you how to develop mental strength and how to focus that strength effectively. It will present you with numerous, real life examples to learn from, as well as giving you a holistic guide to developing mental strength generally. The first chapter gives you valuable knowledge about the different elements that go together to form a strong mind. And this is followed up in the subsequent chapters by a complete **Mind Power System (MPS)**; a 6-step guide that equips you with the mental strength to deal with a large variety of situations. If you follow the steps laid out in this book, you *will* become happier, more successful, more crisis-proof and much more optimistic.

Mentally strong: what it brings you, what it means and how you get there

The benefits of mental strength mentioned in the introduction are only a small part of what you can accomplish as a mentally strong person.

Let's look at some cases of famously successful people. Public figures such as Sylvester Stallone, who was broke and facing homelessness, Thomas Hitzlsperger, who was one of the first footballers to come out as homosexual, or Coco Chanel, who worked her way from a convent to become a world-famous fashion designer, are prime examples of the power of mental strength. There are mentally resilient people all around you too. People in tough jobs that pay poorly. Who, despite the meager salary, are able to provide for their families and even live an enjoyable life outside of work – isn't that admirable? Or, if we take teenagers who are going through puberty while being worried about a seriously ill parent, somehow they still manage to pass their school exams with flying colors, doesn't that deserve the highest praise? What about single parents who have been widowed after the death of a spouse, who do twice or even 3 times as much work as other parents, and still have to explain to their child why the other parent is missing – isn't this also the epitome of mental strength?

Mental strength brings you progress and resilience!

Maslow, in his pyramid of needs, clarified that personal development and self-realization are the only real growth needs that people have.

Each person has their own view of what personal development is but every person will encounter challenges along the way in whatever they do. Whether one starts a family, devotes oneself fully to sports, business or any other pursuit, sooner or later problems will arise. But as you develop mental strength you will make progress through negatively and positively perceived times. Resilience will increase, and you will not break down in the face of challenges, instead continuing on to achieve your life objectives.

In the beginning is the challenge

Challenges, obstacles, and strokes of fate in life are actually defined by your positive or negative reaction to them. *Positive emotions with bad strokes of fate? That's easy to say on paper, but hardly true in real life!* You may be thinking to yourself. For now, you're right. Anyone who learns of a serious illness or loses a family member will definitely not feel positive about it. But while negative emotions are there and have to be accepted, strength can still be gained from these situations.

There are individuals who let life pass them by without savoring it and taking advantage of the many opportunities they have. Then, when they are diagnosed as having only a few months to live, after the initial shock, they finally decide to take advantage of life – in the face of death came the realization that they wanted to live. Furthermore, there are cases in which loss releases unimagined forces in grieving individuals and they suddenly turn their whole lives upside down. For example, a single father and widower who gives his child all the love that the mother had wished for her child on her deathbed; bad fathers transform into model fathers overnight. Bad students who became model students for the sake of their deceased fathers and made a successful career for themselves. Brain researcher Gerhard Roth calls these *teachable moments*: moments that touch a person so deeply on an emotional level, that they are animated to change their previous behavior from one moment to the next.

Example

Christiano Ronaldo is a world renowned football player. He has won numerous national and international titles with clubs he played for. At the beginning of his career, he was a great talent, and his father was proud of him. However, his father died early and did not witness his son's rise to fame. In recent years, Ronaldo repeatedly stated on social media and in interviews that he dedicates all his success to his father. He has even burst into tears on television several times. Even now, at the age of 34 (as of November 2020), which is high for footballers, he is still one of the best in his profession, scoring goal after goal and remaining an absolute leader. How such ambition, discipline and physical prowess have been maintained late into his career can only be fully explained by considering the importance of his father's death. This is a great example of a *teachable moment*.

People who go through these moments are not necessarily always mentally strong. Sometimes they suppress their grief through discipline, which is not healthy for the psyche; but that's another topic. For now, it should be noted that a stroke of fate can strengthen a person's mind and spur amazing and uncanny achievement.

Other challenges that people face in life fit into the description of *self-imposed challenges*. Examples of this are moving home and the resulting new lifestyle, new projects at work or diets for weight loss: In contrast to externally generated, uncontrollable strokes of fate, professional and private challenges are partly self-inflicted. One sees something positive in the challenge in this case, which is why the decision is made to face it. These types of challenges look more harmless compared to the previously mentioned strokes of fate, but they should not be underestimated. For example, the impact of a move on the psyche of children can be significant.

Example

In a study, researchers led by Roger Webb of the University of Manchester analyzed data from children in Denmark born between 1971 and 1997. The focus was on the effects of moving on the children once they reached adulthood. The more frequently moves occurred during childhood, the higher the chances of suicide attempts, mental illness, drug addiction and violence when they became adults. Surprisingly, the parents' financial and social circumstances did not seem to play a role in it, with all of the children being equally affected. Similar findings were made by psychologist Shigehiro Oishi, whose comments were published in the *Journal of Personality and Social Psychology* (2010, Vol. 98). Children who were moved around tend to replicate the same radical changes to the course of their lives when they become adults, especially in the case of children who were moved at the age of puberty.

The conclusion to this is that moving can be a major challenge for people to deal with, and can have potentially strong effects on their future lives. It can be noted that some children also have a different experience and emerge from the move stronger. They learn to adapt quickly to new environments. These and other lessons from the move carry over to later life.

Challenges, obstacles, strokes of fate and other events in life thus put us humans to the test in a variety of ways. Our task is to face up to the challenge as quickly as possible and to find a way of dealing with it. If we succeed in this, we have the chance to grow. By not breaking down and giving up, we demonstrate mental strength. The more often this happens in different life situations, the more we strengthen ourselves in general, so that we can defy an increasing amount of challenges more quickly.

What would life be without these challenges? Such a life would be impossible on the one hand, and on the other hand it would lack a certain charm. Every person on this planet loses loved ones at some point. And if one doesn't lose them because he doesn't have loved ones, there is no social environment surrounding him that makes life worth living. A life without friends and family? Desolate, without support, without succor, lonely...

Even the smaller challenges in life are unavoidable: Sooner or later, every person has to take care of themselves, which is already a challenge with work, cooking, keeping things in order, and all the trimmings. Those who cannot take care of themselves because of an illness have the illness as a challenge.

Despite all this, let's assume that there is a life without challenges and unforeseeable strokes of fate: How could we then still prove our mental strength? Would life still be worth living? This is simply food for thought for you ... left unanswered. Feel free to make your own ideas about it.

The fact is that there are always challenges and strokes of fate that act as a gauge of our mental strength. Those who demonstrate mental strength continue to develop and harden themselves for the further stages of life. The experience gained can be shared with other people, which increases the beneficial aspects to be found in our challenges.

When we talk about strength of mind, we can distinguish it into 2 categories: offensive and defensive. Offensive is when we set goals and move to achieve them. They are challenges that we accept voluntarily. Defensive mental strength is resilience: the ability to catch ourselves after losses and defeats and to respond to unexpected challenges.

Resilience: You feel security in difficult phases

Resilience is the psychological ability to withstand critical situations and crises. Resilient people deal with challenges better than non-resilient people. If they resolve the crisis or continue life in a new way as a result of the crisis, people are considered resilient. The prerequisite here is that they do not let themselves get down and they tackle the crisis comparatively quickly, without letting negative emotions hold them back for too long.

The foundations for resilience are laid in childhood. In his work *Training Resilience* (2020), Max Janson points to the following factors in childhood that would promote pronounced resilience in adulthood:

> ➢ Children have the courage and openness to talk about their emotions.
> ➢ School performance is better than expected.
> ➢ Intact family life.
> ➢ Parents of the children are working.

According to Janson, poverty or wealth would play a subordinate role. If anything, children from wealthy households are expected to have lower resilience in adulthood because they may be "overprotected" by their parents; a factor that stands in the way of resilience. Fittingly, there is a study by U.S. developmental psychologist Emmy Werner that sparked the beginning of resilience research. As part of her study, she observed the development of 700 children in Hawaii who were growing up in poor conditions. What was striking was that despite the conditions (violence, substance abuse, and low levels of parental education), 1/3 of the children grew up to become socially integrated and employed adults. What almost all of these children had in common was the presence of at least one familiar caregiver in their environment who was responsive to their needs.

Whether in childhood or in adulthood, resilience can be trained. The environment plays an important role here because it can teach, strengthen and support. On the other hand, it can of course have a negative influence. In this guide, you will learn how to build a resilient environment. The fact is that resilience is important in difficult phases of life: become resilient and you will find the motivation to live in difficult times!

Example

U.S. President Joe Biden (as of November 2020) has an impressive resume. Despite his political success, he has always remained down-to-earth. Reportedly, since he was a teenager, he still frequents the same diner in his hometown, where he talks to and shakes hands with "normal" people – that is, people who are not prominent or famous in politics. He has served as a senator for about 50 years. He has made a name for himself as a backdoor deal man. He has been able to obtain quite a few betterments for low-income earners and minorities this way. What puts his down-to-earth, successful and people-oriented resume in an even more impressive light is the fact that he has already had to cope with several strokes of fate in his life. His first wife and his daughter died in a traffic accident. He himself was left alone. He started a new family with his second wife. One of his 2 sons from his 2nd marriage died in the war. How was this man able to stand up again and again and deal so exemplarily with Trump's attack in their TV duel when he called Biden's son, who died in the war, a "failure"? He responded matter-of-factly, without bursting into tears or lashing out. The man is resilient! That's why he always found meaning in life and became increasingly successful even in old age.

You grow; maybe even beyond yourself

Resilience is a defensive form of mental strength because it responds to life crises that are not self-made but come about via external factors. In addition to resilience, there is an offensive form of mental strength that is multi-faceted: ambition, discipline, consistency, determination and other factors that spur us to setting goals and challenges for ourselves. Those who set themselves a goal and want to achieve it against all odds, prepare their own challenges. The person in question does this because he or she hopes to gain more advantages than disadvantages.

An example of this would be signing up for a club, taking piano lessons, or going on a diet – a person does not experience a stroke of fate, but makes a conscious decision to take on a challenge. A motive for this could be to learn new things and to expand one's abilities. In the case of dieting, the person might have realized that he has a problem with his body weight, which considerably reduces his well-being and can be dangerous for his health, and thus makes the decision to go on a diet.

These offensive forms of mental strength testify to a love of life. The more pronounced the mental strength, the longer the person sticks to the self-imposed challenge. He or she draws lessons from the mishaps or defeats, improves and starts again. People who have this kind of mental strength are open to new developments in life and have adaptable ambitions. They often outgrow themselves through self-drive because the will is stronger than the potential hurdles.

Mental strength in interpersonal interaction

Mental strength is evident in how one responds to attacks or stands by others in their challenges. Just like in the example of Joe Biden, strong people do not let their emotions control them and attach little or no importance to verbal attacks.

When in the position of helper, mental strength gives you the opportunity to assist others by putting yourself in their shoes. Either you have already been in the same challenging situation as the person you intend to help, or you can draw conclusions about the person's state of mind based on your own similar experiences. In the latter case, there is a so-called transfer performance: You transfer your experiences to other areas of application. Because you are mentally strong, you are able to give people authentic advice and have high credibility. A person who has mastered crises tends to be believed more than people without this experience. By helping others, you are likely to secure help for yourself in the future.

Let's start with interpersonal interactions where you are verbally attacked by other people. They may insult you, put obstacles in your way, or harbor other bad intentions. Either because they are specifically angry with you, or they are angry with people in general. With mental strength, you are 1st and foremost able to not let yourself be swayed from your convictions. Do you remember the introduction that talked about your supervisor criticizing you unfairly? There are cases like that. Mentally strong people deal with it, recognizing that there is a lack of objective opinion behind the criticism. They stick to their convictions and do not attach any importance to the criticism as long as it is not objective: the joy of work remains, and the evening is never clouded by the irrational supervisor. Mental strength in defense against verbal attacks is therefore a question of faith in oneself: Do I believe in my abilities? Am I convinced that I can do the job? Do I believe so much in the path I have chosen that I will "do my thing" with maximum determination? With mental strength, this belief returns.

What does it mean to be mentally strong? What do you need for that?

Mental strength is a kind of cocktail of character traits and situational capacities. There isn't one specific form of mental strength, but different types in relation to the different challenges in life. For example, there are people who are mentally strong only in relation to certain activities. A person who goes to the gym regularly, always puts away the weight plates and leaves everything clean, can have the biggest mess at home.

The subtle differences and many details related to mental strength already give you an initial insight into how to train and develop it. If, for example, you succeed in keeping order at work or in sports, but not at home, then you have a situation-related mental strength. One approach to training or improving is to apply your mental strength to other situations in your life. Step by step you adapt your strengths from work or sports to your home. How this can be achieved will be the subject of this guidebook.

If you want to be mentally strong in as many situations as possible, it is a good idea to reflect on your behavior in the relevant situations and identify personal deficits. Then you work on solutions. The 1st step in the next chapter helps you to take stock of this. It pays to work on individual character traits, because there are specific types of character traits that favor mental strength. To train this "cocktail of character traits", you will...

1. ...select character traits specific to your own life.
2. ...train specific important universal character traits.

A few examples of point 1: A person who gives speeches in front of an audience or plays in professional sports will depend on having "nerves of steel". There is no place for nervousness and stage fright in this situation. Therefore, nerves of steel need to be acquired. People in creative fields require mental strength to deal with customers wishes, even if they do not correspond to their own creative ideas. Teachers depend on having good resistance to student bullying and require a great deal of patience.

Notes on the 2nd point: Universal character traits are motivation, discipline, self-confidence, solution orientation and network orientation.

Motivation

"Motivation refers to processes in which certain motives are activated and translated into actions. This gives behavior a direction toward a goal, a level of intensity, and a sequence of events." — (Stangl, 2020)

Intensity is an important keyword: the more intense the behavior, the greater the motivation. The greater the motivation, the more likely you are to realize your goals. When you want something, you perform more convincingly. The more you want it, the stronger the motivation. A distinction is made between extrinsic and intrinsic motivation: Extrinsic motivation is when you are motivated by another person, or the motivation depends on some other external factor. Since the motivation does not come from you, dropping out is more likely and mental strength against resistance is lower. Intrinsic motivation is when you motivate yourself because *you yourself* want something.

To keep motivation high, you should...

➤ ...know what you really want.

➤ ...derive personal benefit from it.

➤ ...prioritize, so that you offer the greatest focus to what is important to you personally.

Steps 1 and 3 in this book provide guidance in this regard.

Discipline

"Discipline comes from Latin and stands for instruction, discipline and order. Discipline is the act of following rules or regulations. Self-control is called self-discipline." (cf. Brockhaus 1988, p. 553) — (Stangl, 2020)

If discipline means following rules and regulations, then who sets the rules and regulations? Ideally you yourself, which establishes the link to the previous section: self-imposed goals and desires have the greatest motivation, which in turn has a positive effect on discipline. Motivation influences discipline and vice versa, although they are 2 different things. One is motives that justify (motivation). The other is rules that must be followed even without a reason, for example because they are based on social norms or are a basic requirement for one's own life (discipline).

Since discipline does not have to have anything to do with motives, it is often associated with activities that do not suit you. Discipline, then, is the ability to do anyway, something you don't like doing. This ability, in my experience, is often overestimated, but is helpful in the 1st steps and every now and then in between goals. Let's take a thing that is really close to your heart: You like to pursue it, but at some point, there comes an intermediate stage that you are not good at and don't feel like doing. A suitable example would be a psychology course: You love the theory and dealing with people, but the module "statistics" with the mathematical part doesn't appeal to you at all. Now your motivation, which is great in relation to the course of study, but low in relation to the module, is sinking. The catch: You have to complete the module successfully if you want to continue your studies. Motivation is more important than discipline in the whole study program, but in this one module your discipline matters. Are you doing something you don't feel comfortable doing to achieve your big goal? If yes, you've demonstrated mental toughness. If no, you're failing and, despite being highly motivated overall, you've blown the course because of that one module. Too bad.

Discipline is important so that whenever obstacles arise, you keep your motivation high and resist the obstacles. For high discipline, it is beneficial if you...

> ...keep reminding yourself of your motives.
> ...find relaxation in difficult times and reduce your worries.
> ...control your impulses to be less deterred by challenges.

Especially steps 1, 4 and 5 in this book will help you.

Self-confidence/self-awareness

"In psychology, the term self-awareness is understood primarily as self-esteem, i.e., awareness of the importance and value of one's own personality, primarily implying an emotional assessment of one's own worth." — (Stangl, 2020)

Self-esteem equals self-confidence – that's the equation, if Stangl's specialist lexicon, has its way. This equation is plausible in that people who assign themselves a higher value are more stable. Take a person who has already received several employee of the month awards: The awards were given by the entire team and reflect the opinion of all employees as well as supervisors. The person is of high value to the company. With the awards, it is even proven in writing. In addition, the person enjoys his job and even works on optimizing his skills in his free time. Due to the permanent increase in the quality of their work, the person's self-confidence rises. The regularly repeated awards are proof of this. Friends and acquaintances praise the person for what he or she does. Suddenly a critical voice arises, which is not even sufficiently supported by factual criticism. Does it shake the person's self-confidence? Not even remotely. It's different with a person who is criticized around the clock, feels uncomfortable at work and regularly makes mistakes: Here, even the smallest hint of criticism – no matter how implausible – can cause the already battered self-confidence to hit a new low.

Self-awareness means ascribing a high value to oneself. What "high" means at this point is something each person must decide for themselves. In general, it is about feeling important and capable in who you are and what you do. Self-confidence makes you believe in your own abilities or in yourself in general. The stronger one's self-confidence is, the less one's beliefs can be shaken. It can be learned because it grows with the challenges mastered.

For a strong self-confidence and self-esteem, it is significant that you...

> ...surround yourself with people who will encourage you in your goals and desires.

> ...gradually and consistently work on and improve your skills.

> ...with increasing success nevertheless remain grounded, because otherwise self-confidence can degenerate into arrogance.

In particular, steps 2, 5, and 6 in this book will help you with these aspects.

Solution orientation

"Solution orientation is an attitude that helps us in every situation in our lives. Instead of circling around a problem again and again with our feelings and thoughts and researching its causes, we can also simply examine what works well." — (Heller, 2013)

Do not despair of problems but focus on solutions – this is the motto of solution orientation. It thus stands for optimism. Where solution orientation has an advantage over optimism: it is well thought out. While optimism also has the negative blind optimism, a solution orientation is linked to thinking about solutions. The thought process counteracts naiveté. For example, a typical statement with optimism would be, "It'll work out *somehow*." Solution orientation, on the other hand, would ask one of the following questions, in the words of Steve de Shazer's solution-focused brief therapy: "Suppose overnight, while you were sleeping, a miracle happened, and your problem was solved. How would you know? What would be different? How will others know this without you saying a word about it to them?" The answers would be concrete and would help solve the problem.

For a solution-oriented approach, it will help you if you...

> ...live in the present and, starting from your present point of view, determine your possibilities for action.
> ...hold on to your determination and overcome obstacles with thoughtful methods.
> ...accept the current situation and do not act hastily.

Steps 1, 3, 4, and 5, among others, will help you achieve these behaviors and mindsets.

Network orientation

"Good social relationships are vital for people and are one of the most valuable resources for inner resilience. Having a stable social environment, maintaining contacts, and seeking support when challenges arise are healthy behaviors to draw on in critical situations." — (Heller, 2013)

The social environment can motivate and demotivate. It can help or hinder the acquisition of new skills or the improvement of these skills. Furthermore, it has the potential to relieve you of difficult tasks completely in some cases or to assign you additional tasks. Your environment is an exciting thing because it is a factor that you can only partially work on. To a considerable extent, you have to work with what is given; after all, you can't change people at the drop of a hat, and can, only to a limited extent.

Optimization in the social environment comes through your openness and your willingness to make contact. Openness means that you talk about your feelings and don't hide anything. This is because people can behave best towards you if they know your circumstances and your current condition. Suppose you are imitating a strong person: even though you feel weak, people will treat you like a strong person because you give them the impression of strength – more criticism and less praise is usually the result. This is likely to further weaken your actually sensitive attitude. Honesty is an essential input that optimizes the output from others to you. Being sociable as a 2nd factor helps you to regularly expand your environment and make new contacts. This is your key to dynamically adapting your environment to the changes in your life.

Honesty and openness lead you to succeed in your network: Pointless pride should give way to an admission of one's own excessive demands. Help should be accepted and offered in return in order to establish a mutual culture of helpfulness between oneself and other people. With increasing interaction, people become accustomed to each other and learn how best to approach each other in conversations in order to criticize and support constructively, so that motivation and self-confidence are strengthened.

For a successful network orientation, it is beneficial for you to...

> ...value other people and stick to the people who show you appreciation.
> ...openly share your emotions and needs with others.
> ...as your success grows, never forget who helped you achieve it and always remain grateful to those people.

First and foremost, steps 2, 3, 4 and 6 in this book will help you maintain such a network.

Groups of people who can be taken as an example

My experience

For me, it was mainly learning from a model that brought me success. I was able to gain insights into the vitae of numerous people who had been in a similar situation to mine. I learned from their experiences, which saved me from making certain mistakes myself. Certain groups of people excel in mental strength. Due to profession, life circumstances, their own decisions or other factors, these groups of people depend on mental strength for a successful interpretation of their role. They are trained or train themselves to meet daily demands.

As a little inspiration for you, before getting started, I've compiled 5 groups of people that I've taken as examples and highlighted what I found motivating and inspiring about them. The step-by-step instructions in this guidebook have been laid out in the same way in which I achieved mental toughness and would recommend to anyone. Combining that with the 5 groups of people and their regular characteristics contributes to a balanced, holistic approach.

Single parent

Mothers or fathers who are single parents have to perform an overwhelming balancing act. The less independent the child is due to age, illness or developmental stage, the more difficult this balancing act is to accomplish. Either work is done alongside parenting, which presents a time problem. Or the parent does not work and receives financial support from the state, which in turn reduces the financial possibilities.

According to findings from interviews, those who are successful single parents often have the following mental strengths: They talk openly about their feelings and are more willing to seek support. The reason for this is that friends and family more often have to take care of the child because there is no (spouse) partner to support them. Accordingly, the inhibition threshold to interact with other people about various concerns is lowered. Furthermore, as a mental strength, there is a considerable amount of self-responsibility: all decisions regarding the child are made by the single parent. In addition, decisions concerning one's own life and that of the child are made by one's own responsibility. This increases determination and sense of responsibility. Single parents who develop these qualities exhibit strong self-confidence and a network orientation.

Sportsman

Professional and extreme athletes have to withstand psychological pressure. Professional athletes perform in front of tens of thousands of spectators. If you add television, their performances are often in front of millions of people. Extreme athletes usually have nowhere near that many live spectators, but often go to the extent of fighting for survival in their sport. Over time, they harden to such an extent that fear fades out or doesn't even appear anymore. They live fully in the moment and deliver their top performance.

The tragic suicide of former national soccer goalkeeper Robert Enke should prove just how much pressure celebrity athletes are under: He threw himself in front of a train, leaving behind a wife and child. The strain was so great that not even his family could be a support to him. Despite these obstacles, suicides in professional sports remain a marginal phenomenon. The reason for this is that mental training and discussions with psychologists are an integral part of the sport. Fear is overcome. Doubt and pain are transformed into positive feelings. Successes serve as a booster for self-confidence. One's own abilities are consistently worked on in order to improve. Discipline is a matter of course through professional training. Those who are not disciplined will be fined or suspended.

Leaders

Leaders – whether in business, politics, or any other segment – must demonstrate mental toughness when it comes to making decisions with far-reaching implications. Dozens, hundreds, thousands and even more people can be affected by decisions made by one person. It must be admitted at this point that decisions are never made completely alone, because in larger companies and in politics, teams always consult and co-decide. But the final signature and the final decision usually fall on one person. Managers have different levels of scruples. Some don't care a bit about their workers or the population and do what is good for themselves. The others attach importance to the workers and the population and want to improve their working and living conditions. Especially the latter type of leaders, who care about others, can be plagued by pressures, worries, fears and doubts. Mistakes can cause remorse. But everyone makes mistakes. Over time, top leaders tend to realize this, which is why they develop a high level of acceptance toward the current situation – acceptance is a particular mental strength. A solution orientation to improve the mistakes or to further develop the company or the state is fundamental, the network orientation ensures successful cooperation with the consultants and employees.

Warriors / Soldiers

Imagine saying goodbye to your family (parents, children, wife or husband, brothers and sisters, grandparents, etc.) before going to work and not knowing if you will come home alive the next time. Developing the mental strength to cope with this tremendous uncertainty and fear is probably unimaginable for a large percentage of people. The fact that it is unimaginable is not only due to the nature of the circumstances, but also due to the current living situation here in Central Europe. The overwhelming majority of the population was born after the Second World War and has witnessed wars only from a distance. The situation is different in the USA, for example, which has participated in more wars with a larger contingent since the Second World War than Germany, for example. This is not a discussion about whether the military involvement of states or individuals is justified or not. Instead, it should be noted that due to decades of peace in Central Europe, it is often not considered that in other parts of the world it is an everyday scenario that people have to say goodbye to their families and face one of the most feared challenges in living memory: the fight for life and death. Mental training is nowadays a logical part of the education and training of soldiers. In most cases, soldiers are highly motivated because they identify with their home country and want to serve it and the people in it. The motivation and loyalty is so great that they are willing to sacrifice their lives for it – at least that is the ideal scenario. This mental strength, as well as the art of living in the present and maximizing life with family before deployment, are common strengths found in soldiers.

Teen

Teenagers are not to be envied. Although they have far more prospects than adults in terms of age and life expectancy – assuming they are in full health – they find themselves in a complicated in-between world: child or adult – who are they? One relaxing evening, as I was roaming through the offerings on Amazon Prime, I discovered a film (*Chemical Hearts*, 2020) that is, at its core, about a love affair between 2 teenagers that is ill-fated to begin with. In one scene, the problem behind being a teenager is put into fascinating and apt words:

"Think about what it means to be a teenager. [...] Both parents push you to succeed. Your friends push you to do shit you don't want to do. Social media is pushing you to hate your body. It's hard; even if you're a well-adjusted kid from a good family. [...] As a teenager, you're kind of wandering through a no man's land. You're caught somewhere between childhood and adulthood, and the whole world is telling you to be as mature as possible and to please develop yourself. But as soon as you do that, it's, 'Shut up!'"

When the wild dance of hormones is included from a medical perspective, the simple words take on a scientific foundation. Adults can learn a lot from teenagers. Above all, this includes the ability to withstand a storm of emotions and roller coasters of feelings.

The most important things in a nutshell

➤ Through mental strength, one attains better prospects for progress because challenges are accepted and overcome.

➤ When difficult phases of life or crises occur, mental strength helps to find your way back into life.

➤ Mental toughness is also the key to creating a positive environment in which you feel good and make others feel good as well.

➤ Universal character traits that promote mental strength are motivation, discipline, self-confidence/self-awareness, solution orientation, network orientation.

➤ There are groups of people who naturally display mental strength. Some examples of inspirational and usually mentally strong people are leaders, single parents, athletes, soldiers and teenagers.

➔ Observe these groups of people in your personal environment well in order to learn from them and visualize the universal character traits as well as their expression in you! This is how you initiate your transformation into a mentally strong person.

MPS Step 1: Live, Respect and Enjoy the Present

The present is decisive. With dissolute thoughts of the past, you let yourself be distracted by things that you can no longer change anyway. Certainly, it is important to reflect on what has happened and learn from it. This will be a part of this chapter. But it should happen exclusively in designated windows of time so that it doesn't dominate every moment of your life. Instead, you should spend the majority of your moments in the present. Because within the present you work on the future at the same time: Your actions in this moment change the following moment. So, you could say that the present is your chance to create a better past and to shape the future according to your wishes. Thereby, the unconditional focus on the present is purposeful. This is not so easy, because often people get distracted by thoughts. How is the focus concentrated on a certain moment? You will learn this in this chapter by means of exercises and explanations. First, let's take a more detailed look at the benefits of living in the present:

1) Best performance and greatest mindfulness through high concentration

If you let the past distract you, you'll have a harder time delivering a top performance. While you're worrying about outstanding bills, yesterday's disputes, and embarrassing moments, your head will be somewhere else. If you focus on the here and now, you'll perform at your best in the current situation.

That's mental strength: Don't get distracted but clear your head and deliver convincing performances!

2) Capture the beauty of the moment

There is always something going on around you that is worth paying attention to. The couple kissing shows that despite the many conflicts in this world, love still has a place. The girl playing with her dog shows that fun can be achieved by the simplest of means. The well-trained man jogging testifies to the fact that performance is rewarded, and hard work can pay off.

This is mental strength: To renounce the negative influences of everyday life and to discover for yourself the many beautiful and positive things in order to maintain a pleasant view of the world!

3) Gain insights for and about yourself

Only when you live in the present and think about yourself and the things around you can you gain insights that will move you forward. It is very important to think about the past. But what is going on in your mind right now, at this moment in time, in the context of the environment and the current circumstances, gives you the most current insight into your inner self. In retrospect, you never feel as intensely as you do at the moment.

This is mental toughness: to listen inside yourself and recognize what is really important to you in order to use all your resources to achieve realistic dreams!

Living in the present also helps to escape stress. Because stress is the harbinger of the future. The more you think about things you have to do, the more likely you are to put yourself under pressure and be in a hurry. But it should be different... Because while you're sitting on the park bench, for example, and taking time out for 10 minutes, you've decided for yourself that you're going to relax in those 10 minutes. Relaxation can only happen in the moment. Get rid of all the ballast from your head!

With thoughts of the future comes not only stress. Dreams relate to the future. They are an important motivation and incentive to put your plans into action. However, it becomes problematic when dreams degenerate into fairy tale castles. Mastering the balancing act between realistic dreams and concrete goals in life is not easy. Some people don't manage it at all. They build fairy-tale castles while life passes them by – day after day, month after month, year after year. To live in the present means to live one's dreams. An important tool for this is having realistic dreams, which are transformed into stage goals and pursued with the actions of the present.

Expectations, like stress, are the harbingers of the future. They are linked to the condition that you reach a certain goal in a certain time. On the one hand, the problem with expectations is that they can be disappointed. On the other hand, expectations are an important orientation and a benchmark about whether you are on the right track to achieve your dreams. So, what should you do – expect or not expect?

All the topics mentioned and expected results are waiting for you in this chapter. It is the 1st step because the present is your starting point. Become the master of your present situation!

From today the present counts for you

The introduction to this chapter is practical. Exercises are the best way to get a feeling for what living in the present means. By learning step by step to focus on the present moment, you will be better able to understand the rest of this chapter on your path to mental strength. Exercises, aside from helping you focus on the present moment, have several other benefits on the path to mental toughness.

Sport is an element of the following exercises. It helps you develop mental strength in different ways, depending on the sport. If you perform in front of spectators, at best you'll develop nerves of steel, which can also help alleviate or eliminate your stage fright at work. In team sports, you may gain friends who are sympathetic to you. They motivate you and make you believe more strongly in your abilities, which increases your resilience in difficult phases of life.

In addition to sports, special relaxation exercises are useful. One example is Progressive Muscle Relaxation. PME was developed by the American doctor Edmund Jacobson (1885–1976), who was looking for solutions to help nervous people relax. Lowering nervousness is a good sign of developing mental strength. But can PME confirm the hopes? Today the method is well researched. As early as 1994, 66 controlled studies by Grawe et al. showed that PME is helpful as a component of therapies. The greatest effect was found in the therapy of anxiety disorders and psychosomatic diseases (such as hypertension and chronic pain).

The recommendation to you now is to make use of relaxation exercises on the one hand and sports on the other, in order to better switch off and find your way into the present. Below you will find a selection of 3 exercises, from which you should choose only 1 and practice it regularly for a week. In addition to these exercises, it is optimal to try to exercise for 30 minutes every 2 or 3 days. You are welcome to do the exercise in your own home. You have plenty of sports to choose from, just adjust the intensity and technical requirements to your performance level. Try to do this activity every 2 to 3 days for 30 minutes over the course of a month. If you like it, you will increase the frequency and duration of the activity by yourself.

The following 3 exercises are special and serve specifically to focus on the present. Most of the time, the goal is to create relaxation. For you, relaxation is an important element to let the worries and thoughts of the day slip away and to find yourself more easily in the present.

Exercise 1

PME, according to Jacobson, runs alternatively in short or long forms. The short form has the following sequence:

1. Take 30 minutes in a quiet and undisturbed room. Assume a comfortable reclining position. Wear loose clothing. It is best to set an alarm clock so as not to be distracted by looking at the clock.

2. Close your eyes at the beginning of the exercise. Begin to inhale and exhale evenly and at a steady pace.

3. Firmly tense the muscles of the body for 5 to 10 seconds. Then relax for about 30 seconds. Repeat this sequence several times.

In the long form, the procedure is different for the 3rd step. You don't tense the entire musculature of the body, but individual muscles. For example, you start with the hands and slowly work your way to the forearms, then tense the arms completely. After the arms, tense the arms and chest muscles. Continue like this, adding another muscle group to the previous ones, step by step, and in the end the whole body is tensed. There are breaks in between. Feel free to guide yourself through in your mind during the exercise. Tell yourself which muscles to tense and count the seconds. During the contraction you can repeat "hold" several times. Finally, say "release" and relax before starting the sequence again.

Exercise 2

Meditation is a Far Eastern method of sitting in a comfortable posture. The focus is solely on the moment. Any distraction is to be avoided. Beginners are advised to concentrate fully on breathing during the first few meditations. This is to help distract oneself from the thoughts of everyday life.

1. Sit comfortably in a seated position on the floor. Make sure that you are not sitting on your lower legs and that all vessels are well supplied with blood. Otherwise, you risk your legs falling asleep.

2. Sit upright to open your chest and breathe better. Keep your head straight ahead and close your eyes. Let your arms rest loosely in your lap.

3. It is advisable to set the alarm clock here as well. Because meditation is rather monotonous, beginners should practice with a shorter duration, twice a day, in contrast to PME. 10 minutes is appropriate.

4. Inhale deeply at the beginning and hold the air for 1 to 2 seconds. Then exhale again. With each breath, try to imagine yourself going deep into your inner mind. With each exhalation, imagine yourself getting rid of the worries of everyday life.

Exercise 3

The ESA technique is used for emotional stress relief. It is specifically designed for difficult phases of life or stressful moments of everyday life to clear the mind of negative thoughts.

1. Lie down or sit down comfortably.

2. Let one hand touch your forehead very lightly and keep the other hand lightly on your belly button.

3. Close your eyes, breathe in and out calmly and evenly for a while.

4. Now imagine unpleasant thoughts and images roaming through your mind. Hold each thought and image briefly, taking this moment seriously, but after a few seconds of holding, imagine sending the thoughts and images away to distance yourself from them.

If the question remains with you, what influence all these exercises have on the present, it is understandable. To clarify the question, let's first list a common feature of the exercises: They all help you distance yourself from the hustle and bustle of everyday life and the challenges that lie ahead. These influences are replaced by the activity at hand, which usually puts you fully in the moment. In the beginning it will take practice for the meditation, PME or other method to work as they should. With time you will become more and more aware of the present. And now it gets really interesting: Because immediately after the exercise you are usually clearer and more focused in your thoughts. You see the world with different eyes, so to speak.

My experience

I used to try to increase my focus at work by consuming energy drinks. After a few months, I started having problems with my blood pressure. Consequently, I decided to get back to the roots! I renounced substances containing caffeine and taurine. Instead, I meditated, as recommended by millennia-old traditions. At first, I found it difficult to concentrate. However, by focusing on breathing, I had an anchor that helped me shut off all other thoughts. After 15 minutes of meditation, my concentration was better than after several energy drinks. I was setting an insane pace. To this day, meditation is my preferred way to fully focus on the moment.

The focus you take away from these exercises carries over to other activities: At work, you're more focused. In conversations, you pick up on the important little details. You're more efficient when you're studying. When you have to carry out procedures smoothly, you succeed more cleanly. The more often you do the exercises, the more you train yourself to be attentive in general.

Start today and you will succeed in living more and more in the present with each passing day.

Interim summary

Special exercises are the best 1st step you can take to focus your awareness on the present. Through regular practice, you learn to be in the present even beyond the exercises. You'll be less likely to be distracted in your activities.

How you gain insights through mindfulness

Presence requires mindfulness. The exercises mentioned above will help you to achieve it. Continue them regularly to experience lasting change. The more attentive you are in the individual moments of your life, the more insights you will gain about yourself.

Example

You are sitting near the center of a big city park. The weather is sunny and draws lots of people to spend time in the park too. Imagine that your personal mental strength coach comes and sits down next to you on the bench, and asks you the following question, "What's happening here right now? What's going on in the park?" Your answer is, "Nothing." Your coach just shakes his head and says, "That's wrong. In fact, there's a lot going on."

First, it is interesting to determine how a person arrives at the answer "Nothing is going on." The reason is simple: there is nothing "special" going on. Children are playing, couples are kissing, pensioners are feeding the pigeons – all ordinary things for now, things that have been seen many times over already. This is how the answer "nothing" comes about. There are many people who would answer in the same way. But this has nothing to do with mindfulness. Mindfulness would mean observing every detail around you, revealing situations that hold surprising details:

> ➤ The children are playing, but they do it in a completely different way than usual for their age. A child falls and immediately everyone rushes selflessly to help him get up. They put the fun of playing on the back seat.

> ➤ A couple is kissing. But both are easily over 80 years old. Since when has the intimacy shown by this kiss been natural at this age? *Maybe they've even been together since their youth...* You think and begin to develop an interest in the couple's life story.

> ➤ The pensioners are feeding the pigeons, but the horde of youngsters that is approaching is preparing to chase the pigeons away. They run towards the pigeons and drive the pensioners into a rage. What a spectacle!

There is always something going on that is worth watching. And sometimes simple descriptions, like in the 3 bullet points above, hold fascinating details or surprising twists: In the course of your observations, you can, on the one hand, gather insights about yourself, and on the other hand, gain relaxation and improve your mood. You gain relaxation, for example, if you are able to apply this precise power of observation to the shortest of breaks: You don't think about the fact that the break in the office only lasts 5 minutes and that you don't feel like working afterwards. Instead, you're fully in the moment, relieving stress and being soothed while you sit. By being less stressed, you gain more patience, balance, and mental strength.

How can you gain insights about yourself from observation? By mindfully observing the moment with all its trimmings, you begin to think about various things and your attitude towards them. It becomes an automatism. You also get ideas to try new hobbies or transfer observations to the professional context. Being mindful of the moment promotes insights about yourself and what's happening around you. Observations give you plenty of material to question yourself and your current situation. "Questioning" at this point does not mean that your current plans and actions are bad. Rather, "questioning" should be understood as a generally useful action. Because if you don't question whether everything is still going according to your innermost wishes, it can happen that you ignore the dynamic developments of life and maintain your present course, even though a few changes would do you good.

With all that you have now learned about mindfulness, you can already do exercises:

> Use the short breaks in everyday life to observe and think about the things around you. This is an excellent alternative to pulling out your smartphone and stumbling across negative news or other bad influences on it.

> When you are bored in the near future, think about whether there is something to observe. Because as you now know: There's always something going on. This promotes your creativity in many ways.

> Be attentive to people: If you are mindful, you will recognize that your colleague has changed something about his or her appearance. Praise the person to start a conversation with your fellow human beings.

So, mindfulness has multiple benefits. There is one exercise that has the most important function for you personally, the epitome of mindfulness towards yourself in fact. It takes you into the deepest reaches of your consciousness. It brings out thoughts that you unintentionally withhold from yourself. It shows you the path that you really want to take in life. The exercise is: the Inner Dialogue.

In a world full of distractions and permanent accessibility, listening to yourself is worth its weight in gold. The Inner Dialogue helps you to do this. It works wonders and can bring you from the wrong path to the right one or – if you already have the right path in mind – make you stick to it. Inner Dialogue may strengthen your resolve to go through with certain undertakings because it shows that you really want what you are doing and are grateful for it.

Hint!

Gratitude is an essential point in your life anyway. The more grateful you are, the more you remind yourself that you are happy or at least satisfied with what you have. This attitude is balm for the soul. It can alleviate depression and offer support in difficult phases. Also, gratitude suggests to you a certain kind of wealth. It doesn't have to be wealth in the form of money. How about wealth in health, great family, or other benefits you get to enjoy in your life? You will appreciate yourself and your life more with a grateful attitude and be more confident too.

To practice Inner Dialogue, sit down in a comfortable chair, sofa or armchair, making sure that it is quiet around you for the entire duration. Switch off devices that may cause distraction and choose a time frame for your practice. Think about your daily life and about certain aspects of it that are currently affecting you, especially on your thoughts and feelings towards them. Have the courage to question whether what is currently happening is in your best interest. Can you perhaps change something in your favor? Ideally, at the end of the Inner Dialogue, you will realize that you are happy with everything you are doing. The purpose of the Inner Dialogue is to intensively deal with yourself. When you are done, recall 5 facts for which you are grateful and repeat them several times.

Exercise

Conduct the Inner Dialogue as a ritual regularly at fixed times. Keep a diary of your thoughts as it allows you to trace your emotions back several days, weeks, months, or even years, giving you a solid overview of your development.

Interim summary

Live in the present to be mindful of the many stimuli and wonders around you. They inspire you and change your present for the better if you let them. Through Inner Dialogue, also be mindful of yourself to find out if you like the present in its current state.

Realism and fairy tale are clearly separated

The principle of the Inner Dialogue helps you to distinguish between realism and fairy tales. Based on your insights, it will be easier for you to set realistic goals and have realistic dreams. It becomes clearer to you where you stand and what you can expect.

Consequently, you don't build fairy-tale castles that make you live in a dream world somewhere other than in the present moment.

Example

You are currently in debt but you dream of being a millionaire. The fairy tale dream in front of your eyes, makes it difficult for you to see the small, realistic steps necessary to reduce your debts first. Because as long as you have debts, you have to pay the high overdraft interest or reminder fees, and you cannot find your way out of your precarious situation. Your dream castle is also your prison at the same time. Through the Inner Dialogue, you remind yourself that you want too much and you realize that it's better to think in small steps. In this way, you will eventually work your way to being debt-free, whereupon you will have more opportunities to invest your money profitably. This is the way you are most likely to become a millionaire. But dreaming of being a millionaire at this point would be counterproductive. You have to get out of debt first.

Inner Dialogue promotes insights, but on its own does not guarantee that you will quickly escape from the fairy-tale castle. For this, you need other methods too. And here's just the thing:

Exercise

1. Write down everything you dream of – even the most absurd things. Take your time, using the Inner Dialogue in a quiet environment.
2. Now write down how much time you have available every day and how much of it is lost for duties that you *have to*

perform. How much time is left for the realization of your dreams?

3. Check whether it is realistic to realize your dreams in a timely manner with the time available to you and your other resources (e.g., money, your own abilities, health condition). Stay away from dreams that are far beyond your time and other capacities. Cross them off the list. In the Inner Dialogue you will probably discover several little things that are attractive substitutes for unrealistic dreams that have been crossed off.

4. The list should contain dreams or rather smaller goals that you can realize in a relatively short time with your actual resources. These smaller goals may be related to a big dream and bring you closer to it. Just make sure that they can be achieved in a timely manner and that they are not so far away that the journey seems long and arduous. Make it easy for yourself!

5. Create a step-by-step sequence with your stage goals to tackle the realistic dreams. The more you achieve, the closer you will get to your bigger dreams. Update your goals regularly; especially when you reach them and new goals are needed.

What is useful in this context is to take a cue from people who already achieved their dreams. Which person is suitable as a role model? What can you learn from other people in relation to your individual stage goals? Celebrities, people from world history, people from your circle of acquaintances and others you can think of can be included. The advantage of people who are in your immediate vicinity is their availability: unlike celebrities, they are available for conversation, so that an individual approach to your needs is possible. This process of seeking out and orienting your-self to role models is known as "learning from the model". It is a psychologically recognized method in which it is only important that you choose models who are in a similar situation to you. For example, a person who has not had to struggle through life as you have, but has had everything laid at their feet, is not a suitable model for you.

Gretchen question: What does all this have to do with life in the present?

For one thing, setting realistic goals and moving away from unrealistic dreams promotes a connection to your current situation. If you orient yourself to your current situation and create concrete plans for your future actions, you are most likely to be successful. Setting good plans already means, to a certain extent, living in the present.

Second, scrapping unrealistic dreams helps you live in the moment. After all, you don't have the distraction of dreams that are unlikely to come true at this point in time. Instead, you devote yourself to realistic goals that you actually approach – precisely because they are realistic and appropriate to your current situation.

Take a book or a hard drive as an example: you need to leave as much info as possible for a person to master the challenges ahead. The hurdle is that both book and hard drive have limited space for information. Do you choose to leave info about work steps that are 8 years in the distance and don't currently matter? Or do you leave the person with information material that starts with his current situation and shows him step by step the way from here to his better future? Rather the latter, isn't it? So, think of your mind as the hard disk. The fewer dreams or things that lie in the distant future are stored in it, the faster and smoother the hard drive runs.

Interim summary

Your life today will be positively influenced by banishing from your mind everything that currently has no relevance. Dreams are not forbidden, but they should be realistic. Then you will be more motivated, focused and most likely to deliver a good performance in the present.

Expectations are important, but only belong in the present to a limited extent

Expectations play a basic role in the present because they concern the future. You don't expect anything from an event that has already happened. You may have an expectation of the outcome of the event that is taking place, but that is still in the future and could distract you from the present moment.

Example

You have an important performance in front of an audience. But while you are delivering it, you are actually thinking all the time about how it's going to turn out and expecting it to be a good outcome for you. The problem here is that you distract yourself with your expectations, resulting in confusion or mental lapses.

This being said, you may have noticed that at the beginning of this subchapter that I said expectations play a *basic role* in the present, because they concern the future. So, what is the appropriate way to deal with them?

Expectations as a guide

With all the focus on the moment, it must not be disregarded that expectations can serve as orientation. They are identical to goals or smaller milestones you set for yourself. For example, if you have a milestone goal to be more disciplined in completing your work or study assignments by the end of this month in order to have more free time, your expectation is that you will achieve that goal. So, expectations have the role of giving you a direction.

If you had no expectations, you would have no goals.

If you didn't have goals, you would have a harder time motivating yourself.

If your motivation were low, the likelihood of success would decrease.

You realize at this point that expectations used appropriately, serve as a benchmark for determining your success as you set milestones to achieve a larger goal. These milestones are associated with the expectation of mastering them.

What if this expectation is not fulfilled? Then you haven't reached your milestone either. As a consequence, you might make course corrections in order to avoid further failure. So, expectations in this sense help you to monitor your successful progress.

Expectations should not be completely discarded. Because expecting something from the next 3 months in order to assess your own performance is beneficial. Accordingly, the crux of the matter is not whether you have expectations, but *when you have expectations.*

Have expectations – this is the right way to do it!

Imagine you are sitting with your best friend in your favorite café. You haven't seen each other for several months and you are having a chat. One topic that arises is your plans for the future. You talk about your upcoming bachelor thesis. Your goal is at least an A average, because you believe you have the necessary qualities, you are normally pretty good in your studies, having an A average in previous subjects. Now think for a while and decide whether it is an appropriate expectation.

The answer is that it's absolutely an appropriate expectation – it is a goal that you set for yourself. It only becomes problematic when you allow yourself to be distracted by your expectations in the present while you are actually performing a task because you should be free to focus on the moment. Applied to the example of the bachelor thesis, it means that while you are working on it, at best you don't waste a thought on your expectation. Otherwise, you will distract yourself, make careless mistakes or even bigger errors, be unable to think clearly and risk your A-grade.

My experience

I used to be a talented soccer player. If I had understood back then how mental strength is developed, I might have had a great career. But that's a thing of the past. What matters to me is that my expectations on the pitch got in the way. In training sessions and several hours before the game, I formulated expectations and set goals. That was good. But the problem was that on the field, I kept thinking about the expectations and let them take me out of the moment. I worried about not meeting the expectations every time I received the ball.

Situation	Orientation guide	Distraction
Sports: You have a game.	If you set training goals and expect to achieve them, it's productive.	When you're playing, you're thinking all the time about whether people are rating you the way you expect them to. You're distracted by that.
Social / Love: You are dating a person for the first time.	You formulate a plan for the interview before the meeting to make it interesting and be prepared for questions.	You're sitting across from the person, thinking all the time about whether you're coming across as charming as you planned. Because of these thoughts, you are not in the moment and unable to listen to the person.
Job / School / Study: You carry out a project.	You set a plan for the stages of the project and work through them according to your expectations.	During the project, your thoughts revolving around the outcome will get you off track.

Expectations are orientation and distraction at the same time. They are an important orientation if they show you the way in the present and a distraction if they distract you from your task. Therefore, formulate expectations, but do not let them dominate your mind.

Interim summary

If you have expectations and they are disappointed halfway through, you are condemning the moment. This takes you away from taking the minimum chance of success. Therefore, when performing a task, always stay in the moment without expectations. Deal with expectations and their evaluation when you have the time and peace of mind to do so.

MPS Step 1 in brief

> ➤ Great attention should be paid to the present. Because the past is over, and you should leave it behind. The future, on the other hand, cannot be influenced and should be approached without fears or queasy feelings.

> ➤ By focusing on the present, the past is let go of and the future is shaped. Because the best way to live the life you dream of in the future is to act purposefully in the present.

> ➤ Useful exercises to develop sensitivity to the present and greater focus on the moment at every stage of daily life are PME, meditation and ESA techniques. Sports, gymnastics and breathing exercises of any form are also helpful.

> ➤ Whoever lives in the moment and pays all attention to the present, gains many insights about himself and his surroundings, making it clearer what his wishes are and how he would like to live.

> ➤ By focusing unconditionally on the present, distractions are reduced: Expectations, worries, fears and other hindering thoughts occur less or not at all. Therefore, the present principle helps you to perform at your best.

➤ Concentration on the moment, reduces stress levels. Resulting in better mental balance and relaxation, which can also improve health conditions.

➔ Living in the moment leads to concentration. Concentration makes you forget your own weaknesses. So ultimately the present principle provides mental strength!

MPS Step 2: Know your value

Not badmouthing yourself or one another is an artform in life. Badmouthing is an easy trap to fall into, when any person can research information online and be a know-it-all. It is admirable and commands the greatest respect when you can discover a person's value despite their flaws. Or even better is discovering the value of a person in their flaws!

> ➤ Overweight: Ever heard of the artist Peter Paul Rubens, who artfully staged female curves and made them fashionable? In the past, for example during the Renaissance in Central Europe, a plump body was considered a symbol of prosperity and performance.
>
> ➤ Knowledge gaps: Every gap is an opportunity to gain new knowledge and enrich oneself. Many smart people have fewer such opportunities because they think they already know everything or feel less incentive to learn.
>
> ➤ No money in the account: It doesn't matter. Because you certainly have other strengths. Maybe you're eloquent. Maybe you have an incredible amount of knowledge. Maybe your wealth of experience can't be topped. And by the way, if you don't have any money in your account, you can't lose any...

Everything that is negative also has a positive side. Everything that is positive also has a negative side. You decide which side you want to see. Of course, it should not be ignored that some situations are an exception to this rule. If you always look only at the positive side, you run the risk of hiding from things you need to improve in your life. This chapter, therefore, does not teach you to always look through rose-colored glasses. It teaches you the ability to exercise a healthy measure of appreciation and criticism towards yourself as well as towards other people.

Developing appreciation requires clear reference points

Appreciation doesn't come from anywhere: it must be based on the recognition that a person has value. The more convinced you are of a person's value, the more appreciation you will have for him or her. To put it simply, you need reasons to value a person:

> ➤ Does the person have certain physical or mental abilities that demand recognition and respect?
> ➤ Does the person have character traits that speak for him or her?
> ➤ Has the person succeeded in achieving certain goals on his or her resume?

These points are easy to understand up to this point. Should a person have trained his memory to be photographic, then he deserves appreciation. If the person has succeeded in completing training, he also deserves appreciation for it, regardless of what kind of training it is. Here is the crux of the matter: an academic who has completed a course of study and may even have a doctorate is held in higher esteem in the eyes of many people than a person who does track construction work on railroad tracks. The academic is considered to have a higher value. A reference point is taken on the basis of which the person is judged.

Do you know which people will most likely make the most intriguing acquaintances and make others feel better about themselves?

Individuals who see the specialties in what appears to be the least prestigious profession and recognize that this profession must also be learned.

People who are willing to go beyond initial uninteresting aspects to further explore the interlocutor and discover impressive details in the course of conversation.

People who are capable of being enthusiastic about any kind of special circumstances that distinguish another person.

These insights apply when thinking about yourself, and to conversations with other people. If you try to open yourself to the details of every single clue, you will recognize even in the simplest professions, the simplest activities and the finest character traits why every person is special – and should have their strengths valued!

My experience

In a phase of life when I was not succeeding at anything, I denied my mistakes and criticized other people. I was so meticulous in my criticism that it was unbearable. So, it was no wonder that almost my entire environment turned away from me and showed me little appreciation. A vicious circle of lack of appreciation developed, with which I and my entourage beat each other up. My dissatisfaction almost degenerated into depression. When

I took distance and practiced writing down positive things about myself and others and repeating it several times, there was a change in my mindset. People were surprised at how respectful and benevolent I became toward them. As a result, they almost automatically showed me more appreciation as well.

Connection between optimism and appreciation

Appreciation is best developed when you approach things with optimism. Optimism means positive thinking. If you believe that something will turn out well, you are in an optimistic mood. If you think optimistically, it will be easier to see the value of a person or thing even where it is hard to see. The reason for this is that the optimistic person views the world through a filter of confidence, enthusiasm, and love of life. This filter leads to a more willing engagement with other people and their finest qualities. An optimistic person will be able to see something good even in the weaknesses of the interlocutor or in his own flaws.

Example

You're having a hard time with math class. Luckily, you have a teacher who cares about his students. He gets on the level with his students by trying to understand what life is like for a teenage person these days. The confusion of hormones during puberty, the expectations of home and teachers to be an adult and face challenges – these things and more make it difficult to always deliver a top performance. Then, when one subject doesn't suit you – in this case math – the barriers to good performance are all the greater. But the teacher is an optimist. He believes that he can get a few percent more out of you. He comes to this conclusion because of your good performance in physics, which is partly similar to math. He devotes himself to you more intensively and tries to create parallels between mathematics and physics. In the process, he gives you a smile or 2 in appreciation and deliberately makes a mistake himself to take the pressure off you.

What principles about appreciation do you learn from this example?

1. Optimism is what drives you and makes it easier for you to develop appreciation.
2. Getting on the same level as people and not appearing aloof is elementary to getting through to the person. To do this, it is often necessary to try to put yourself in their shoes.
3. A smile helps because it gives familiarity and warmth. It is a positive way to express emotions. It makes you approach people in a sympathetic way.

Appreciation is not an art. It only needs signs or characteristics by which you can assign a value to a person. Every person has these characteristics. If you think optimistically, you will find them most easily. Just as these rules apply to your behavior toward other people, they also apply to your thinking about yourself.

Exercise

Now it's time for you to show appreciation for yourself. If you have not been doing well so far, this exercise is of utmost importance. If you have been giving yourself appreciation so far, this exercise will help you to give yourself even more appreciation.

Write down all of your personal characteristics – both positive and negative: external features, physical abilities (including those used in work or sports), mental abilities, character traits, your resume (from birth to now), and other things you can think of. Go into great detail. Write down one personal characteristic on each line. Leave space for more text next to these characteristics on the right side of the list.

Next step, write down everything positive that is connected with the respective characteristic on the right side. If there is nothing positive, leave it alone. But don't give up too soon if you can't think of anything. For example: You don't tend to finish anything, instead you are always starting new things. This superficially negative characteristic has the positive accompanying factor that you like to try new things. Being open to new things is by no means an attribute that everyone has. It can open up more scope for you because you come into contact with new things, impressions and experiences. So, congratulate yourself for this!

Lastly, try to find ways to use the positive sides of the negative thing to your profit. It will help you find out your strengths by focusing on your positive traits, and may even directly create solutions to problems that have been bothering you for a long time.

The consequences of appreciation

How does appreciation lead to mental strength?

It should be noted that appreciation makes you consider yourself or others to be more important. Being important strengthens people, because it provides a reason to live. If you were not important, a large part of your motivation would disappear. This can be related to the whole of life, or individual parts it. Someone who is not wanted in a family because of a quarrel, or a misunderstanding may be made to feel unimportant. That person loses a significant amount of support in life. The same scenario is conceivable at work. Imagine a person helps build a company for 30 years and then suddenly gets fired in exchange for severance pay on the grounds that he or she can no longer lead the digital transformation and align the company in a modern way. Such a scenario is not unlikely. Being sidelined and deemed unimportant hurts one's own esteem. This steals your motivation; perhaps even the general motivation to live. With esteem, the exact opposite results:

You are important!
You are needed!
Your qualities are known and recognized!

These words are balm for your soul. You gain more self-confidence. With more self-confidence comes courage. Because when others need you and count on you, your skills are special. You're more likely to dare to take a risk and you increase your chances of success because success requires a certain amount of risk-taking.

If you use the knowledge you have gained to make the connection to the last chapter, then you will notice that appreciation will give you a better present. This happens in several ways:

- ➢ You recognize your value and abilities, which reduces the amount of distracting negative thoughts. This makes it easier for you to focus on the moment.
- ➢ Self-awareness and confidence will make you more confident in your skills, which will help you with current performances.

> ➤ You are generally freer in your mind. Because where there are no worries and negative emotions, there is more room for absolute freedom of thought.

The more appreciation you show people, the better they feel. They begin to like your company. They may adapt your point of view so that you build each other up and keep each other happy. Appreciation based on reciprocity is a wonderful breeding ground for building pleasant interpersonal relationships. You gain in the form of contacts who value you, or interlocutors who are a support for you in difficult phases. In this way, mental strength also comes to you from the outside.

Interim summary

When you value yourself and others, you gain confidence, courage, self-esteem, and uplifting social contacts. All these resources strengthen you mentally and help you to build a mentally strengthening environment. This environment not only helps you, but you also help the people in it.

Tell yourself and it will be!

Up to this point, you have recognized the positive things about yourself and your fellow human beings. That is already enough to encourage appreciation towards your fellow human beings. But it is not yet enough for appreciation towards yourself. In simpler words: If you express appreciation in some way to your fellow human beings in conversations or chats, you have already done your best to get along well with them. Your job is not to play therapist and keep telling them how important they are. In the long run, that can seem too pushy. If a person asks you for help or expresses self-doubt, you are welcome to talk to them more often and encourage them. But otherwise, the appreciation you suggest in passing conversations is perfectly sufficient. You suggest this appreciation by smiling, showing interest in the topics the person is addressing, and generally keeping an open attitude with a bit of praise in between. It's different with yourself, though. Since you are reading this, you've probably identified some mental improvement needs in yourself. If you realize that your problems lie in low self-esteem, the lessons in this chapter so far will be of some help to you, but only a little. The important thing is that you keep working through the lessons. If you have noticed – to use the previous example – that an open attitude towards new things is your strength, you should remind yourself of this regularly. If you don't, you will most likely remain at the same level as before, and instead of positive openness, you will see your lack of perseverance as a negative aspect. After all, you are used to a negative self-perception in your mindset. Negative must become positive! The best way to do this is to change your mindset.

Notice

Changing your thoughts from negative to positive, from failure to success, from pessimism to optimism is an essential part of my book *Habits of Winners*. In this title there are a dozen exercises to program your thoughts towards positivity and success. By reprogramming your thoughts, you work on your subconscious mind. The subconscious mind is a collection of automated processes of both thought and action. They run automatically because you have become accustomed to them. If you succeed in shaping the automatisms in such a way that you think positively and act accordingly, then you take a decisive step towards success. The reprogramming of thoughts also works in connection with appreciation.

A useful exercise to help you program your thoughts for self-esteem works through affirmations. Affirmations are positive beliefs. The trick is that you repeatedly remind yourself of your strengths. Again, following on from the example earlier, an appropriate affirmation would be, "I am open to new things." This belief system can be continued by pointing out the advantages of your openness: "I always tell people about my new experiences. In conversations, I'm an interesting grab bag. People like me for that." You convince yourself of your strengths, until you no longer think of yourself as someone who abandons tasks. The mental strength is inside you. You just have to bring it to the surface!

Exercise

Based on the previous explanations and examples presented, you should now have a number of strengths on your list which you have derived from your weaknesses. Just as a lack of staying power has become a commendable openness to new things, you can find something positive in all your weaknesses. You write these positive insights as beliefs on another sheet of paper. Use one sheet of paper per belief. In order to keep paper wastage low, you could divide an A4 sheet into 2 or 4 smaller sheets. Stick each sheet somewhere in your home with adhesive tape. One sheet could be hung opposite the toilet and the other on your refrigerator for example. While another could be great on the inside of your front door. Ideally, you should be confronted with these affirmations several times during the course of your day. Take your time to read the respective belief when you see it, even setting a specific time slot every day to read it aloud repeatedly for 10 minutes. You will get used to thinking of the strengths naturally over time.

Developing appreciation for yourself takes practice. Writing down and repeating positive beliefs is only a 1ˢᵗ step, comparable to a map or a navigational route. You see there is a path to becoming confident, but that path must be walked.

Interim summary

Formulate beliefs. Write them down on several pieces of paper. Hang the notes in your home in frequently visited corners and confront yourself with them. Repeat them over and over again, even as a ritual at fixed times of the day. Over time, you'll get used to making your thoughts positive.

Caution. When is it too much appreciation?

Can there be too much appreciation? It depends entirely on how appreciation is practiced. Basically, appreciation does not mean praising oneself or others to the skies. Appreciation in general is a positive, respectful and benevolent basic attitude. Praise and recognition are instruments that serve among a multitude of other instruments to express appreciation. But they are not necessary for expressing appreciation. If they are used too frequently and excessively, praise and recognition are even dangerous. They carry the risk that weaknesses are ignored and problems are not perceived. This is the answer to the question of when it is too much appreciation: when it is used in an overdose.

What the overdose is depends on the individual context. A good guiding formula for you is: If you notice that appreciation contributes to further development and an improvement of the situation, you are doing everything right. If appreciation prevents you from developing further because you look at every problem through rose-colored glasses, appreciation is too high a dosage. Because the example in the last few paragraphs was used frequently and followed step by step, it is worth going back to it again:

Is it dangerous if you notice a lack of staying power in yourself, but ignore this weakness by substituting an openness to newness as a strength?

Yes and No. Completely "ignoring" weaknesses is never good. You should always have your weaknesses on the screen and observe them carefully. The exercises in this chapter were not designed to eliminate weaknesses from your consciousness. They were designed to help you focus on your strengths *first and foremost*, to motivate you and make you optimistic. But you should still observe your weaknesses. In this sense, the answer to the above question is: If you ignore the weakness, such a form of appreciation is dangerous. But if you keep the weakness on your radar and critically examine it regularly to see if the positive mindset has improved anything, the appreciation is not dangerous.

If the meaning of the word "appreciation" is analyzed precisely, it is never dangerous. But for an adequate explanation of what appreciation means we would have to write a whole book on the topic. For now, just practice it and discover for yourself through experience.

Interim summary

Appreciation – despite all the focus on positive thoughts and strengths – does not mean disregarding one's weaknesses. The goal is to no longer let weaknesses dominate one's thoughts so that they shape one's mental state. A regular critical examination of personal deficits remains essential for further development.

Physical well-being for more appreciation

The calculation "Physical well-being + mental well-being = appreciation" rounds off this chapter. Because mental well-being exerts the greatest influence on appreciation, it had the largest share of attention. You are urged to continue the list exercises and affirmations. They are the most important component of expressing appreciation to yourself and also giving a sense of appreciation to others.

Physical well-being has an influence on self-esteem. It also makes pain, discomfort or lack of concentration less likely, enhancing your mood and performance. A particularly good physical condition (as you might have after a wellness weekend) has the potential to contribute extraordinarily to a sense of overall well-being. People achieve this through things like massages, sauna sessions, vacations etc. These special treats can be a great reward to offer yourself. But when are rewards appropriate? Mostly when one has accomplished something that deserves a reward. Rewards like this are often associated with appreciation in the subconscious mind. So, when you reach for a reward, it may automatically activate the feeling of appreciation in you. Accordingly, rewarding yourself with physical wellness measures is beneficial for self-esteem in more ways than one. Be careful not to go too far though. They should not noticeably harm your finances (massages, for example, are costly) nor discourage you from working on yourself. These types of measures should always have a special value, otherwise you will get used to them over time and the self-esteem gained will decrease. So, use these measures sparingly, but under no circumstances give up doing something good for your body once a week or once every 2 weeks for a few hours. Healthy nutrition, sports and moderate exercise as measures of physical well-being may of course be practiced more frequently than massages, because they are a permanently important contribution to human health.

Interim summary

Physical well-being influences self-esteem less than mental measures, but it is also an influence. Regular measures to increase physical well-being and a permanently healthy lifestyle promote your self-esteem.

MPS Step 2 in a nutshell

➢ Strengths and weaknesses are a matter of opinion. Every strength brings with it weaknesses. Likewise, every weakness brings strengths. The goal is to focus on positive personal characteristics.

➢ Positive thoughts about oneself and others lead to appreciation. Appreciation does not mean blindly praising and closing one's eyes to weaknesses. Instead, it is about adopting a respectful, benevolent and positive attitude.

➤ Those who adopt such an attitude while still working on their personal weaknesses, are charting an optimal course in life.

➤ Appreciation contributes to more self-confidence. One's own abilities are implemented confidently and offensively, which is an important factor in delivering the best performance and being successful.

➤ When there is appreciation towards other people, there is a high probability that one will be perceived as sympathetic, liked and also appreciated. Through reciprocity, positive human relationships and conversations occur, which strengthens one mentally.

→ Pay the most attention to your strengths while being aware of and working on your weaknesses. Meet people respectfully and benevolently. This is how the appreciation principle helps you gain mental strength!

MPS Step 3: What you really want, you will do!

Determination does not mean that you want something. Wanting is a possible initiator of determination, but it is far from a guarantee of it. For example, you may want to lose weight in order to reach your dream weight. But isn't that what many people want? Yet they fail because of the obstacles; because they are not determined – because determination means pushing through against resistance. You know the resistances beforehand and prepare yourself for them to achieve your objective anyway. Or unexpected resistance arises spontaneously, in this case, too, you know no ifs and buts, because you are determined.

Determination can do little with phrases such as "would like to have," or "should really have." Determination knows little to no compromise. If you make a resolution, you put the intention into action. If you live in the present, confidently make a plan, are self-assured, and block out all obstacles through determination, you will be mentally strong. In this chapter you will learn what it takes to be determined. By means of the insights and exercises, you will train your determination directly.

If you don't want or need to, don't!

A lack of determination can even have dangerous consequences. The best example of this is provided by Bernhard Moestl
in his work *Shaolin – Du musst nicht kämpfen, um zu siegen* (2008). In
it, he describes the preparations travelers make for trips to dangerous parts of the world: they would plan to carry a firearm with
them to defend themselves in case of attack. But those who had
never pointed a gun at a person before would not consider that
pulling the trigger requires determination; after all, you are taking
a person's life... Most people would still possibly draw the gun, but
few would pull the trigger. The attacker, on the other hand, might
become aggressive at the sight of the gun. At worst, he would
seize the weapon and use it against you.

This example, which uses a life-threatening situation to
demonstrate how important determination is, can also be applied
to more banal circumstances:

> ➤ A degree graduate has received a brilliant job offer. In ad-
> dition, he has recently obtained his driver's license. Since
> he is not a "normal" novice driver, but a driver with very
> good earnings in his new job, he decides to finance a
> sports car via leasing. The only reason for him to get this
> car and not a good mid-range car is the approximately 400
> hp. He just wants to "let his hair down" on the weekends
> and race along the roads. As a novice driver however, he
> doesn't even begin to take advantage of the vehicle's
> power and speed. He lacks the courage to fully press the
> gas pedal. Now he has leased a car that is too expensive
> and to which he is tied for 2 years.

Lack of determination has the potential to make purchases of luxury and equally ordinary items redundant. It should be considered beforehand whether one will be determined to wear the eye-catching garment, to fully exploit the potential of the sports car and to perceive other margins.

➢ You have a very good friend. You both get along great. There is a whiff of love in the air. The catch is that the person ended a relationship a few months ago and is mourning the former partner. The person is attracted to you but is not really ready to start something new. However, you convince them to try anyway. In the end, the relationship that has developed is partly forced. You both knew deep down that your friend's openness to a new relationship was not (yet) complete. From now on, everything you do, as well as the relationship itself, is accompanied by indecision: the sexual interaction, the conversations, the activities, every single hug. The relationship is breaking down, and the negative experiences have put rocks in the friendship's path. Nothing is the same anymore.

People should be honest and trustworthy in their relationships. The relationship – in whatever form – should be completely voluntary. Only in this way does each person feel comfortable in their role. Accordingly, the distribution of roles should be precisely communicated and considered in order to interact together with determination and full dedication.

My experience

I had a very good friend who I was in a relationship with many years ago. The subsequent friendship lasted for 5 years. In the meantime, the woman was with another man. She was young and it was only her 2nd relationship after me. The man was what in colloquial language is probably called a "bad boy": criminal record, aggression, insults towards other people. However, she gave herself to him completely. After the relationship ended, she was never the same. I noticed in our conversations that she was still mourning him because he had always been good to her. She was not over him I could tell. Nevertheless, a few months after their breakup, I suggested that we try getting back together again. I hardly had to convince her because she remembered our previous relationship and our good friendship. The relationship broke up after a few months though, because she was still thinking about her ex. She wouldn't let me touch her; we couldn't talk to each other as openly as we had in our friendship. She had entered into a relationship she was not ready for – and I myself had known it deep down. In the end, it was no wonder that we separated quickly. The determination had been lacking; especially on her part because she longed for her ex. My pity, which drove me to want to be with her, was also not a good driver for determination. It was extremely questionable of me to burden the friendship in this way in the first place. To this day, we have hardly exchanged a word since the breakup.

Buying things, interpersonal relationships, making decisions in life, organizing one's free time; ideally, everything is done with determination. The examples show why: determination leads to consistency. Consistent actions, in turn, favor the realization of one's qualities. This is where the uplifting connection to the last 2 chapters comes in: You are at this moment pursuing a task; your focus is optimal, and you are fully in the moment. Because of your self-esteem, you feel good and confident in your abilities. Because you are pursuing realistic goals and are fully confident that they are in line with your desires, you are determined. This determination leads to more enthusiastic actions. The stronger your determination, the less you pay attention to even the most stubborn obstacles (e.g., fear, negative coaxing from others, past failure etc.).

There are 2 factors that favor determination: Wanting and needing. *Ideally*, you do what you have to do in life. Taking children to school, going to work, studying, caring for sick parents or friends etc., are usually things you have to do. If you notice anything about these examples, it's that they're usually linked to "wanting" too. Don't you want your children to go to school because you want them to learn and grow up educated? Don't you want to study in order to have a financially secure life later on? Don't you want to take care of your parents because you love them, and they have always taken care of you?

The fact is that we have to do these things. But "have to" alone is not sustainable. Imagine if you only imposed duties on yourself in your life and consequently only did what you had to do. Man is not a machine. A purely compulsory program risks burnout, depression, and other mental and – depending on the type of activity – physical illnesses. Some things have to be done, but important in life are the things that are a combination of "must and want" or pure "want". In the case of "having to and wanting to", there are more and more attractive incentives to pursue a thing because of your will. The stronger the will and the greater the incentives, the stronger the determination.

Wanting has one challenge: You have to decide. While with "must and want" or pure "must" you are usually relieved of the decision by external factors, it is different with pure "want".

Example

What is certain is that you *have to* work. Only a few people, because of their wealth or age do not have to work. The majority of adults do. However, what job you do is decided before you go to college, university, or generally when you choose a job. You may have limited choices, but when choosing, you ideally still decide what you *want*. The challenge is freedom of choice.

So, for all decisions where you have complete or partial free will and multiple decision options, you are literally spoiled for choice. This problem is greater today than it was several decades or even centuries ago. In the past, one's career or life path was to some extent pre-defined. For example, it was not unusual for young men to continue their father's profession. Young women were not infrequently – in the English aristocracy of the 19th century, for example – forced into marriage. Marriages were supposed to have benefits and, ideally, to create new wealth. In the past, there were fewer options. This was rarely good, because life was to a large extent determined by others.

Nowadays, at least in Central Europe, the opposite is the rule: you are faced with an abundance options. In the digitalized world, which is rich in perspectives thanks to networking, people tend to find it more difficult to choose. While there is financial and educational inequality in Germany, there is no denying that numerous support programs offer a wealth of prospects on a silver platter to young people from a wide range of social classes. Study abroad with Bafög as financial aid? Voluntary social year? Taking a sabbatical year after school, earning decent money and then traveling the world? This is how the wheel of seemingly endless possibilities turns for many people. Somehow, some people then prefer to have it all; namely...

> ...become an influencer on social media and make a living with a few posts.
> ...manage life with a family of 4 on the side.
> ...follow the main profession, because as an Influencer they don't yet earn enough.
> ...but a degree program would also be exciting, which after all can be planned flexibly as a distance learning program and doesn't even require a high school diploma.
> ...in addition, there is the diet, for which you would prefer to cook fresh every day for 3 hours.

All at once? Impossible. But even those who have fewer options and enjoy few privileges in their lives still have more options than people in the same situation several decades ago.

Now it becomes important to remember the first step – namely the present principle. Because as you know, the present shows you what is realistic in your current life situation. The list you just made of things you would like to do all at once is an example of what can be possible. The things individually are not unrealistic. But to do everything at once *is* unrealistic. Due to an overload, the individual goals gradually break away because they cannot all be pursued consistently with your time capacities. Overload and lack of prioritization are often a reason for lack of determination. In this sense, we create the connection to the 1st step; that is, the 2nd chapter: You remember the exercise from the 1st step, which was about realism and fairy tale castles? Pull out the list again. You set realistic goals in the exercise based on your time capacities as well as resources. These, because they are realistic, are achievable for you. But are you really determined to achieve them? **Check it!**

While "wanting" something (a goal) promotes determination, it does not equate to more determination. If you simply want but are not determined to put in the necessary effort (e.g., physical work, mental work, money, patience), "wanting" is more of a burden to you than a help. Wanting without determination – it's like working without full dedication. You are not realizing your potential. You are also more likely to get distracted. Now is the time for you to continue working with the list from the Realism Fairy Tale exercise in which you formulated your goals. You need to identify the goals that you are really determined to achieve.

Exercise

Think about which of the goals you wrote down you could have achieved long ago. For which goal have you already made several attempts, but never followed through consistently? Consider whether it was due to a lack of determination or the wrong approach. If you can't think of an alternative approach and you have doubts about achieving your goal, you are most likely not determined. You probably lack the last bit of motivation to follow the goal. Therefore, put it aside, if possible, and examine all other goals. Ideally, the end result is that the list includes your realistic goals, measured against your desires and dreams. You are determined to achieve those goals. Determination is characterized by the fact that you don't put things off and you follow through consistently. If there is a lack of execution, you are at least creative and find different approaches to try. This is how determination shows itself – not through perfection, but consistent and creative work on your own plans.

Interim summary

Wanting and needing, as well as the mixture of both, are beneficial for your determination. But they do not guarantee decisive action. Therefore, shorten your plans around those things that you are not willing to overcome all obstacles to achieve.

With determination comes mental strength

Determination is directly related to mental strength. For one thing, it gives you confidence. When you're determined to do something, you're sure you'll see it through. This security prevents you from questioning yourself unnecessarily. The questioning is over – you have already done that with the previous exercises and now you have realistic goals on your list, which you will actually carry out! Internalize this thought: *"Everything that is on my note with goals, I will really carry out!"*

This unshakable thought means determination. In addition to certainty, determination gives you consistency in action. You can no longer be dissuaded from an action during its execution. The present principle learned from the 1st step is better put into action.

Example

Maybe you know a little bit about tackling in soccer. Imagine 2 players running towards a ball and trying to win it. One player is from a team in the champion's league while the other is from a team that was relegated. The champion has a pure winning mentality. He knows what he wants, and based on last season's titles, he knows he can do it. The player from the relegation team is intimidated just by the look on his opponent's face. The 2 players get closer and closer to the ball, accelerate and slide in. The champion is fully determined and follows through. While there is a hint of doubt in the other player's mind, just enough to take away his speed and strength for a split second and prevent him from getting to the ball first.

Determination is evident in you. It's the expression you have on your face at work while presenting a project in front of several people and arguing for its implementation. You stand in front of the audience with bright eyes and verve that your solution/concept is the best. People see your determination and trust you. Determination also means attraction. It makes you attractive and opens up opportunities for you to build a following or at least a social environment.

Closely related to your determination are discipline and motivation. Discipline, in particular, is a factor more closely associated with mental strength than probably any other. Discipline promotes your determination. It ensures – as you may remember from the definitions in the 1ˢᵗ chapter – that you are able to follow self-imposed and externally dictated rules. Following self-imposed rules is called self-discipline. If you don't feel like doing some-thing, but you remember the rule and as a result you do the activ-ity, you are disciplined. The more pronounced the discipline, the more unshakable your determination. Discipline is the protective wall around your determination. It leads to you holding on to your goals in the face of adversity. By regularly repeating your motives, you call your dreams to mind. Visualizing or aiming for realistic dreams strengthens your motivation. The more motivated you are, the more determined you are. It seems to make sense to strengthen these 2 components together. Three exercises for each will show you how.

Increase discipline with 3 exercises

Exercise 1

So far you have worked on plans with the help of this book, but not yet on rewards. If you allow yourself rewards in your stage goals – the extent of the reward must match the level of difficulty of the stage goal – then you will increase your willpower. You know that a reward is waiting for you while you are working on one of the milestones so it pays to be disciplined and stay disci-plined. Assign appropriate rewards to your milestones now. Again, use the present as a benchmark and do it in a realistic way.

Exercise 2

Go after tasks that you don't like. Think of 5 things that can be practiced regularly, but you don't like. Of course, these tasks should make sense and move you forward in some way. An ideal example would be dusting. Start with 1 of the 5 actions and prac-tice it for a duration that seems reasonable. Over time, increase the duration and gradually add the other tasks too. Through this exercise, you will condition yourself to have a higher "pain tolerance" to unwanted tasks.

Exercise 3

Get into the habit of keeping order in your home, your workplace, and any other place you visit. Order in the outside world rubs off positively on your inside. By keeping your surroundings tidy, you lay the foundation for discipline. Because if you keep seeing before your eyes in black and white that you live tidily, it will be easier for you to believe that you can do other things consistently as well. *As on the outside – so on the inside!*

Increase motivation with 3 exercises

Exercise 1

Think as if you have already achieved your goal. When you think about a milestone or a big goal, always say to yourself, "I have... accomplished." Be careful not to get sloppy and think you don't have to do anything. Use this exercise sparingly, e.g., as an addition to the beliefs. Say the sentences to yourself a few times a day in your mind or out loud.

Exercise 2

Keep a diary of your successes. Diary keeping has celebrated a resurgence under the Anglicism "journaling" anyway. More and more people are open to journaling and no longer label it as an activity for romantics. Be one of them and keep a journal of your progress! If you like, you can keep it in bullet points and concise.

Crucially, if you experience a drop in determination, have a booklet you can look into to remind yourself, *"I've made it this far and I'm going to keep making it!"* This sounds simplistic, but it definitely works. Therefore, just do it and be amazed!

Exercise 3

The 45/15 rule is that you do a task for 45 minutes and then take a break for 15 minutes. During this break, you can do your mindfulness exercises or anything else that is dear to you. All that matters is that you take the break. The fact that you only have to do a task for a limited period of time increases your motivation. For tasks that you don't like but are shorter in duration, you can of course shorten the 45/15 rule. For a 15-minute task that you absolutely hate, working for 5 minutes and taking a 3-minute break might have a good effect. Just try chunking the task and working towards your goal in a relaxed manner. Unfortunately, this rule will not be feasible for a professional job with prescribed working hours. Understand that it is not universally applicable.

Interim summary

Determination makes you mentally strong. Outsiders notice this strength in you. You develop your maximum potential. Work regularly on your motivation and discipline to keep it that way.

Accept obstacles and gently remove them from the way

You may encounter obstacles on your way to becoming more determined. Depending on the area in which you want to be determined, you may be confronted with various resistances. As Dr. Thomas Späth and Shi Yan Bao recognize in their guidebook

Shaolin — The Secret of Inner Strength (2011), accepting the obstacles is important. By accepting them, you become aware of them in the first place and can work on clearing them out of the way. If you ignore them, on the other hand, you run the risk of failure due to head-in-the-wall tactics. When faced with obstacles, the authors recommend focusing first on the reason for their occurrence. Every obstacle has a positive intention: fear, for example, serves to protect people. Convenience prevents people from consuming too much energy.

You have the choice to fight the obstacles rigorously: Possibly you acquire an additional guidebook for overcoming fear in order to fight the obstacle from all sides. But is this the right way? At the very least, it is not the path that is most likely to lead you to success. After all, a lack of compromise and a rigorous approach carry the risk that you'll overextend yourself. What about compromise?

> ➤ If you feel fear, meet it halfway by first accepting its protective function and then looking for ways to gradually free yourself from it.

> ➤ If you consider yourself lazy, admit to being lazy, but gradually reduce it. Also, try alternatives to laziness, such as massages. Again, you're relaxing and just lying around; but with the difference that you're doing something good for your body and — there you go again after the last chapter — showing yourself appreciation.

> ➤ If you see your environment as a hurdle, reduce contact with people who you think are counterproductive for the development of mental strength. Or tell them directly that

you hope for more understanding or respect from them, depending on where you see the deficits.

Dealing with obstacles is about acceptance and in finding creative solutions. Surely you understand that when 2 people share a journey, a problem, or a task, they must coordinate in order to act in unity. An association of 2 people where each person acts as they please would be indecisive. So, it is with you: Several different versions of "you" live through your thoughts, i.e., the inner critic, the optimist etc. They express themselves in your characteristics, strengths and weaknesses. Sometimes one person dominates, sometimes the other. Developing mental strength and determination means finding a consensus between your different inner voices. When you succeed in this, you concentrate all your strength on the task you are performing and go about it with determination.

Finding compromises between your desires and obstacles is the best way. How do you find the compromise between fear and performing in front of an audience, laziness and an upcoming task, nervousness and ambitions for a successful exam, habit of snacking and targeted diet?

Exercise

Behind an obstacle there is not only the bare negative blockage, but also the positive intention. The exception is your personal environment, because you can't know why others put obstacles in your way. There can also be a positive intention behind it, but this is not certain. With your environment it helps to take things with a touch of distance *or* to address problems openly. But with the obstacles that arise from within yourself – your individual mental weaknesses – positive intentions are also hidden. Write down your obstacles and also note what positive intention could be hidden behind each one.

In the next step, think about compromises: For example, consider how you can tackle the fear gradually without setting yourself mammoth tasks. For arachnophobia, 1 option would be to get close to spiders, by a meter or smaller increments at a time. For claustrophobia, you would have the option of starting in a larger room first and then moving to an increasingly small one. Laziness is your weakness? In this case, you could put together a program where you only have to get up to do 1 thing for 1 minute on the first day. Over time, you increase the duration.

Taking small steps, being careful, responding to obstacles and incorporating them into your planning – that's your path to determination. Each step away from the obstacle strengthens your overall mental fortitude and makes you more determined. It is helpful to enlist the help of trusted people.

Finally, it should be noted that compromises require dynamism: For example, if you notice that overcoming an obstacle is much easier than you planned, increase the pace. If you've bitten off more than you can chew: It's no big deal – just take a step back and approach the whole thing more cautiously. What is important in all these points is a basic measure of patience. No obstacle disappears through thoughtless actions. As in the 1st exercises and in your life in general, you should look at yourself in the present and always question how you can best eliminate obstacles step by step with the current means at your disposal and your present attitude towards the obstacle.

Interim summary

Obstacles are accepted. They are not an unconditional enemy but have at least a small positive background. Compromise and adjust step by step with this positive background and your goals until you have eliminated the obstacle. If other people are the obstacle, then have a clarifying conversation or distance yourself from these people.

MPS Step 3 in brief

➤ Being determined means wanting or needing to do a thing while having the willingness, means and methods to remove all obstacles.

➤ The important initiator of determination is the "want" or "need" or a hybrid of both. The "want" should dominate in your life and activities so that you feel joy and fun.

➤ In your list of realistic goals, commit to the things you are really determined to do. Set your priorities so that you pursue these things first and foremost.

➤ Through determination, you pull other people along and win them over – whether as friends or in some other role. In addition, you carry out your actions with the maximum use of your potential.

➤ Motivation and discipline strengthen your determination. Do special exercises regularly, such as journaling, and bring order into your life to strengthen your determination.

➤ Accept obstacles and compromise on their removal. In this way, you will gradually and gently get rid of them without overextending yourself.

→ Acquire the determination to make the most of the present! Through determination you live more consistently in the moment and can thus let go of negative emotions and focus on the positive in the present.

MPS Step 4: Reduce your concerns!

Reducing concerns, like determination, is a result of living in the present while at the same time being an important support for remaining in the present. When you are more serene, you make sure that the personal problems of life do not dominate you. Attention: Although in the following we will talk about serenity; it isn't the same thing as doing nothing. It is simply about letting problems get to you less. This does not mean ignoring your problems, but instead tackling them at the appropriate times. Working on your solutions at the times you can, want to, and need to. Otherwise, you concentrate on other things.

The connection with this and the rest of the content in this book is that serenity acts as a calm antithesis to decisiveness and guards against actionist tendencies. It ensures a balance in your plans as well as your actions.

Dealing with minor concerns: Are they the laughs of tomorrow?

In life, there are both major and minor worries. In this chapter, we will start with minor worries – because the burden on the mind is the lowest and the worries themselves are sometimes even completely unfounded: In science, the distinction between major and minor worries is made on the basis of the thesis that major worries have the property of assuming pathological proportions. They permanently restrict attention, lead to higher alertness in phases of relaxation and literally torture the mind: they are transferred to other situations, which in many cases can lead to a generalized anxiety disorder.

Minor worries, on the other hand, are trains of thought that do not permanently haunt you but do bother you in certain situations. Possible examples of such minor worries are:

➢ Failed date with a person from work: the next time you meet this person, you will probably sink into shame – such is your worry.

➢ Stress with the boss: your boss was raging about your performance one day. He yelled at you about something or other seemingly every half hour. You're worried about how to deal with him next time and what consequences there might be.

➢ You got a bad grade, and you have to confess it to your parents, who are always very strict in such cases.

➢ You have to give a presentation in front of a large audience, but you have put on slightly transparent clothing. You are not aware of this before the presentation, but only realize it shortly before the end. You rock the rest of the presentation confidently across the stage and disappear afterwards. My goodness, that was embarrassing! You are still concerned about it, days later.

All these little worries, if you read it that way, are mostly temporary; "mostly" because there are exceptions. But we won't dwell on that now. As a rule, these worries are unfounded. The confession of your bad grade, the stress with the boss, the lecture, and the date are over – what reason is there to worry anymore? There could possibly be consequences, but if we think about it, these things are so trivial that they have happened to every person: For example, if the person from work complains about the date, the audience might agree with him, but just as well know that not every date goes well.

If you think about it, all these worries could have a positive ending: What if another person from work, hearing about the failed date, would learn more about you and think that you are an interesting person. Soon, the person approaches you, you set up a date and it goes well. What if your supervisor complained about you to the CEO of the company, but the CEO couldn't understand the criticism and would transfer you to a better department?

These positive consequences are not probable, but they are certainly possible. What is definitely not possible, however, is for these small worries to result in a serious negative consequence for your life. They are mostly irrational worries. Accordingly, it is hardly surprising that, with time, they even become laughs among family and friends.

Exercise

Find such small worries in yourself. Preferably, look for worries that are coming up in you at the moment; perhaps something embarrassing happened to you a few days ago that is causing you worry. You may also dig around in the past and recall embarrassing situations or minor disputes in order to learn for your future with the help of this exercise. Write down all the minor worries you can think of. Now write down at least 3 reasons why these worries are unfounded or even ridiculous. Common reasons are that you will never see the person again anyway or that they are normal mishaps that happen to everyone. Then imagine how you will later laugh with other people about exactly these worries.

My experience

In my life, I have often been thwarted more by small worries than by big ones, which is extremely paradoxical. I was able to deal quite well with big worries like high debts that I couldn't pay off in the meantime. I just dealt with it as long as it was necessary and worked to find solutions. But minor concerns where my livelihood and health were not threatened came up regularly in my memories. I think it was because the stage was set early in my childhood for such reactions: Time and again, the embarrassment of minor mishaps had been emphasized by my mother, so I had acquired that mindset. As life progressed, experience gave me the realization that minor embarrassments are perfectly normal. They are normal and often show in a funny way how imperfect we humans are. This imperfection in minor situations is what makes human charm.

Dealing with major concerns that threaten life, livelihood and future

All types of major concerns require impulse control and acceptance. This is evident even in the most extreme emergencies. For example, when a person has a heart attack, he usually feels it keenly. The severity of this stabbing pain is usually such that a person fears for his or her life. In first aid, it is recommended to calm the person down. Paramedics on the scene do the same. Calming creates control. Breathing is then slower, so there is even a direct medical effect.

However, in emergencies and in the case of particularly great worries (e.g., financial existential worries, worries about the health of a loved one), there is no need to deceive yourself. With previous exercises for control and regular practice, the effect is usually manageable. Emotions and impulses that cause emotions are best controlled when you train specifically for them. For this it is indispensable to prepare yourself with exercises.

By the way, you should never underestimate the effects of human emotions. Because the human brain usually reacts emotionally. The very way the brain works means that the first thing to switch on is the limbic system, which controls the emotional part of the brain, among other things. If you don't develop control over emotions, you risk the emotions controlling you. Where this leads depends entirely on the situation. There have been people who have hurt or even killed others because of a strong emotional reaction. Apart from these extreme cases, there are numerous other situations in which a lack of control over your emotions can harm you: this can be the case when you worry.

Worry is a deep emotion. If you are afraid of a spider, you are *afraid*. If you are afraid for someone dear to you, you are *worried* about him. *Worries are characterized by their long-term nature.* They enter your consciousness regularly and roam your thoughts. Worries can result from single embarrassing events, where they are small and irrational worries. You learned this in the last subsection. These worries are usually tomorrow's laughingstock. It is different with worries that result from deeper concerns, such as:

> ➢ Poor health with unpredictable consequences for one's life.

➤ Financial problems and lack of clarity regarding one's livelihood.

➤ Problems at school, college or work and not knowing if they can be solved.

These 3 examples are united by uncertainty: you don't know how they will turn out. This poses a problem for you; namely, the fact that you cannot react decisively. You are caught between hope and realism. Uncertainty interferes with much of what you have learned in the past steps of this guide.

Let's take a situation as a counterexample in which the outcome is clear: In this example, you are aware that someone dear to you has only 3 months to live. The uncertainty is gone. Slowly, the worry about what will happen to the person also fades. Other worries take their place, such as how the person will cope with the situation and how you will manage life without them. However, you have the time to cognitively process these things slowly with the person and find solutions. The fact is that uncertainty is intrinsic to the existence of worry. You can rarely eliminate this uncertainty. Often it disappears by itself, in the sense of "time that heals all wounds".

Or you accept the uncertainty. This is exactly the point that always helps with major worries: to accept the existing uncertainty because it cannot be influenced. Based on this acceptance, you rethink your current situation (step 1) and determine how to react to it decisively (step 3). In order not to let your emotions overtake you despite the uncertainty, it is necessary that you control them and the impulses that lead to emotions. Max Janson, in her work *Training Resilience (2020), states* that a high degree of self-discipline is required to control impulses. Otherwise, you'll let yourself get out of control.

If worries occur for the first time, then a new assessment of the current situation is necessary. The 1st step in this book will help you to do this. Afterwards, it is important to decide to take a certain path despite the worry and to follow it. Self-discipline helps you to do this. You motivate yourself by demonstrating why you should continue to live and give your best despite the great worry. One possible motive would be to keep going to make the loved one on the bedside proud. In order to accept the new life situation with determination during periods of great worry, the impulse control and acceptance exercises described below are useful.

Three exercises to develop acceptance

Exercise 1

Because the death of a loved one is something that causes great worry and comes to every person sooner or later, Exercise 1 is specifically dedicated to this case. The worry of losing a loved one can be alleviated by making the most of the time with that person. If the person is willing, spend as much fulfilling time with them as possible. By the way, this also applies to yourself: Should you receive bad news regarding your own health, it helps to make the most of the time you have. In the book *Resilienz trainieren* (2020), Max Janson appropriately refers to an interview with Ottfried Fischer, who suffers from Parkinson's disease: Fischer does not want to despair about his illness. Instead, he set himself the goal of only doing what he enjoys. Making the most of remaining time and resources – that is the motto of this exercise. Time well spent also distracts you from the worries that plague you and/or your loved one.

What if it's already too late and you can't spend any more time with your loved one because, for example, they're already dead? In this case, memories help: Remember every moment you spent with the person. Remember your pleasure with other people. You will realize that the beautiful memories will calm you down.

Although intended primarily for coping with grief, this exercise is also useful for other types of loss. For example, if you fail with a major professional project, you can cling to the excellent experience afterwards. From this you gain courage and confidence for the present. Your exercise, then, is either to spend more time with people dear to you or to use memories to show yourself that you took full advantage of the time without worry.

Exercise 2

It is difficult to see the sense in it when one is plagued by great worries. But there have been numerous people who have found strength in difficult phases of life. They developed a way of looking at things that explained to them the reason for the problems. Explanations are the basic building block of acceptance. When you receive explanations and develop understanding, you will find things easier to accept over time. So, start looking for explanations: Is it possible that life wants to test your strength in this way? Is it possible that someone wants to make you aware that you have made big mistakes and need to change something in your life? Should you spend more time with that person from now on?

Whatever explanations you find: Try to convince yourself and derive an action from it, so that you accept the problems and gradually free yourself from your worries.

Exercise 3

There are good times and bad times. At the moment, bad times may prevail – but that will not always be the case. On the one hand, think about your own life: What crises have you successfully survived so far? How did you feel afterwards? On the other hand, look at other people, whether on television or in reality. People will be an example to you of how to act in your situation. By learning from past experiences and learning from the model – that is, learning from other people – you may find your way to accept.

Three exercises to control impulses

Exercise 1

Great worries can lead you to rash actions. You have no patience to wait for a result. You have to do something. Patience is therefore a 1st helpful means of gaining impulse control. It is not uncommon for individuals to resort to complete irrationality when they are worried. The student who can't keep up swallows Ritalin. The grieving family man flies his sick son to a faith healer in Honduras and spends a 5-figure sum. In both cases, there is probably no improvement. The risks, on the other hand, are quite high. So, learn to take a little time out in situations where worry overtakes you. Allow yourself 10 seconds to let the worry enter your thoughts. Worry and count down the 10 seconds. Afterwards, sit down and write a pros and cons list to find out which actions are really worthwhile in this situation. This is how you learn how to make rational decisions.

Exercise 2

Find a release valve. During difficult periods in your life that cause you anxiety, find an activity where you can let out all your emotions. Classic examples are the punching bag at home, the gym and jogging. In all 3 sports, you can let off steam while varying the intensity: running faster, punching harder, lifting more weights. Professional dancers and musicians are able to use dancing or playing music as a release valve. Some people, on the other hand, swear by doing household chores as a good emotional release valve. Your release valve is unique – so find the right one for you and use it. By shifting your emotions into an activity, you power yourself down and lower the risk of being overwhelmed by worry. You're more likely to deal with your worries in a rational way.

Exercise 3

Talk. Your environment is important. Talk to people – especially those who share your concerns –about what is bothering you. This way you will all gain support and understanding. Several people together also find more ways than a single person to identify a way to deal with worry. Difficult situations usually bring physical closeness: a hug here and there, maybe a little cuddling. This stimulates the release of happy hormones, which soothes one's aggrieved soul. Openness also promotes interpersonal relationships. Opening up to a familiar person encourages that person to open up as well.

Interim summary

Great worry brings with it the essential problem of uncertainty. Uncertainty causes you to be divided between the possibility of a positive or a negative outcome. Learn to accept this and control your impulses to act thoughtfully and rationally.

Slowness beats haste

"Slowness beats haste" – this does not apply to all areas of life. In a sprint, for example, only the person who is the fastest wins. Haste is indispensable in this case. But already in a marathon over a distance of more than 50 kilometers, things look different: If you hurry at the beginning to be 1st for as long as possible, you are not dosing your forces properly. However, dosage of forces is the be-all and end-all when it comes to long distances! Intimidating the other runners over an impressive 10 kilometers will do you little good if you run out of breath in the remaining part of the race. The principle of slowness can therefore even be applied to sports. Consequently, it is important to think around a corner or two: Essentially, the principle is about taking your time with certain things. That's the way it is with worries in particular.

As you learned from one of the exercises earlier, actionism is a risk of making the wrong decisions due to lack of patience and deliberation. Especially with deep problems, a slow approach to finding a solution is beneficial. How slow should it be? As slow as your individual situation allows. The challenge with difficult life phases or profound problems is that they are often a comprehensive construct. Multiple factors need to be considered:

➢ If the person dies, who will take care of the children?

➢ What happens to the person's estate?

➢ Who pays for the costs of the funeral?

As inappropriate as these trains of thought may seem, where the passing of a loved one is concerned, they often play an essential role in the subconscious of people close to the sick person. Those who write down the individual accompanying problems and prepare in time are most likely to be mentally strong. Imagine that you not only take care of the sick person before his or her passing, but that you create a schedule that tells you when to take care of which bureaucratic and organizational aspects: in this case, you will not be overwhelmed by the duties after the person's death but will have organized everything in advance step by step and will be able to deal with the grief after the death in peace. You can slowly work through everything and slowly process the grief without being rushed by bureaucratic aspects and the like.

The goal should be to eliminate major problems and worries in your life. For this purpose, you put other goals on the back burner for the time being and develop a plan to solve the new challenges. Through the plan you prevent actionism and solve the problems thoughtfully, because you take time for their solution. Despite worries, simply continuing your life as before is like a suicide mission. You will be overwhelmed.

Another advantage of slowness is that a phenomenon known as serendipity may occur. Serendipity means finding solutions without looking for them. Life is dynamic, as you have learned. Something is constantly happening that can affect your life against all expectations. If you act rashly and make rash decisions in your desperation, it is possible that when solutions fall into your lap, because of your previously rash actions, the problems will have piled up and it will bring you less.

Bernhard Moestl also expresses the benefits of slowness and composure in his bestseller *Shaolin – Du musst nicht kämpfen, um zu siegen* (2008). Both factors would help to reduce mistakes and control emotions. As a result, problems or worries would not grow, but solutions would be most likely to emerge.

Interim summary

Get into the habit of looking for solutions slowly, especially in the case of big worries. Hasty, impatient actions usually increase the problems or overwhelm you. By thinking before you act, you determine a sustainable and promising course of action.

MPS Step 4 in brief

> ➢ There are small worries and big worries. The small worries are often the little mishaps and embarrassments that befall us in life and sometimes occupy us for a surprisingly long time.
> ➢ Get into the habit of seeing events that lead to small worries as a normal part of human imperfection and put them to rest. Often you can laugh about these worries with a little time distance.
> ➢ It becomes more serious with major worries that threaten existence, health, happiness and other elementary components of life. These worries must be taken seriously.

➤ The best way to deal with the problem of uncertainty in big worries is to train your acceptance and optimize your impulse control with the exercises described.

➤ When you look slowly for solutions to big concerns, finding sustainable and optimal solutions is more likely.

MPS Step 5: Work on your skills!

The 5th and final step of mental strength work is based on developing your individual skills. In the 6th step, a slightly different program awaits you. It is no longer about building mental strength, but about how to handle it optimally. This chapter is, in a way, the last step on the way to mental strength. So, mobilize your full attention once again to continue the consistent work on yourself. Up to this point you have worked with mental factors, now you switch to practice: By promoting your individual practical skills, your mental strength will also benefit. *How does this work?*

Let's say you play an instrument: you've practiced several pieces and play most of them flawlessly. There is already a problem here that you can work on: *most of them*. Playing the piece *mostly flawlessly is* not enough for 100 percent confidence. Because when you have your performance, you can't be sure that there will be no mistakes. This fosters stage fright and anxiety. It complicates your focus on the present moment, calls to your attention the stern and expectant looks of the crowd, and deprives you of 100 percent determination in individual movements of the fingers on the piano or breaths on the trumpet.

Your program so far has helped you to optimize these aspects in particular:

> ➤ Living in the present helps you block out the audience and their expectations to better focus on performing correctly.

➤ Appreciating yourself will help you feel more confident about your abilities and how to deal with mistakes. If you become unsure or make mistakes during the game, you will probably be able to handle them better.

➤ Through determination, you perform your music game with more confidence and trust in your abilities, so the likelihood of making mistakes decreases.

➤ Composure helps you pay less attention to the watching crowd and not put the audience on some kind of pedestal. They are human beings who also make mistakes. With this mindset, you feel less pressured.

All of that helps. But what about being able to play the instrument and the pieces so well that you don't have to concentrate on them at all? Imagine if you had such a strong ability that you could wink at the audience and talk to them while playing – all at the same time, without thinking, worrying, fearing, doubting, lacking confidence or any other hindrance. The reason for this is your abilities, which are so trained that they cannot be shaken. You know no failure because you have mastered things by heart.

About the benefits of skills

The most comprehensive skills possible are an advantage in different contexts. Even if you are disrespected and bullied by people, it can help you to work successively on improving your skills. Suppose you are being bullied by other people and you have a desire to develop more mental strength against it: Bullying in today's times is no longer a classic student or employee problem, if it was ever limited to those groups of people at all. Nowadays, even teachers and supervisors are no longer immune to bullying.

Everything you've learned so far in this book will help you deal with bullying better. The skills you practice in this step will leave their own mark: they will enhance your reputation in the eyes of others by improving your skills and giving people less reason to bully you. Please don't think at this point that you would be guilty for bullying – not at all! Also, it should not be your goal to change yourself to please other people. But if there is a chance to improve yourself and thus to completely overcome the few mean arguments for bullying, and – this is the most important thing now – this is in line with your interests and goals at the same time, then take the chance!

Basically, training your skills is a potential cure for anything:

➤ You can silence critics and bullies by convincing them with new or expanded qualities.

➤ Doubts, fears, stage fright and other kinds of worries give way to the certainty that you have things fully under control through your skills.

➤ The more skills you perfect, the more transfer and linking you can do, so you learn other things faster.

➤ You gain more confidence in your strengths and are more likely to achieve your goals.

➤ Stress levels drop because you overcome challenges more easily, saving time for other things.

There are various models of the human being. These models are regularly used in psychology and business. One model that in my opinion represents today's times well is the human resource model, which sees the human being as a pool of different abilities and skills. First and foremost, in business this model plays a major role. It has led to the emergence of a lot of motivational models, such as Maslow's pyramid of needs, which was already introduced at the beginning of this book. The goal in the human resource model is to promote and develop a person's individual abilities and skills. Maslow's pyramid of needs explains why:

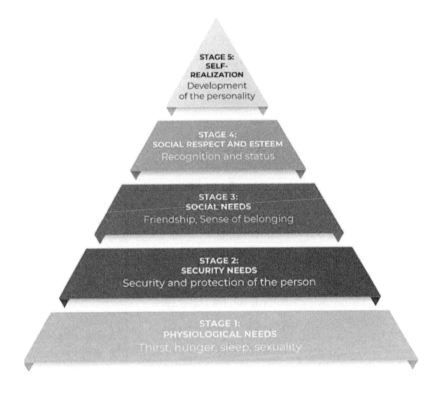

Need satisfaction takes place in order from bottom to top. First the physiological needs are satisfied, then the safety needs, then the social needs and esteem. Last but not least comes the need you are dealing with in this chapter: the development of your abilities, the unfolding of your personality and thus self-actualization. The importance of working on your own abilities is also clear from the closer classification of needs: the first 4 levels are considered deficiency needs. This means that the desire decreases with the degree of satisfaction. Only when the needs have not been satisfied for a certain period of time do they return. But it is different with the 5th stage and the development of one's abilities: These are the growth needs. According to the assumption, these are not satisfied with the extent of satisfaction, but increase. In this, the model reflects the human urge for constant further development.

So, you're not just working on mental strength in this chapter. This chapter is a kind of link to your whole life. It links mental strength with self-realization and also links self-realization with the human striving for more. Striving for more in turn leads to more meaning to life: no matter in which situation, no matter at which age and no matter in which context – your life will never be boring this way!

Interim summary

Continuously practicing your skills and acquiring new ones contributes to a better mental state and more resistance to bullying as well as other negative influencing factors by strengthening your competencies. Moreover, working on your skills favors self-actualization in the long run.

What skills and resources do you need?

The list of your goals serves as a very detailed template for this subchapter, which you have worked through precisely in the previous 4 chapters. You have formulated your personal goals precisely, subdivided them, prioritized them and checked them for feasibility according to your possibilities. With this list of goals, you now check which skills and resources you need. You train the skills or acquire them in the first place. Resources, on the other hand, you acquire. They are means that you buy, produce or otherwise bring into your possession. Sometimes even mundane resources can make quite a difference.

My experience

When I was a child at school, I was bullied. In fact, the blame did not lie with me. Because bullying is the fault of those who practice it. But I gave these people several reasons to bully: My hair was long and since it had no volume and I didn't care about my styling otherwise, it hung over my eyes. In addition, I had a mustache, which seemed rather out of place in the overall picture. My clothes were loose and partially hanging off my body. It was thrown together fashion. Every person has the right to maintain this style! I myself would not mob a person because of it. But what distinguishes a mentally strong person is, even when wronged, to think in several directions. Personally, at the time, I considered that a change in my style might do me good. Secretly, I admired my "cool styled" classmates. The injustice I suffered from bullying animated me to rethink: I had the ability to change visually. But the willingness was missing. The willingness changed somewhat when even my few friends told me to change my appearance. In essence, the "bullying mob" seems to have been right somewhere... This is exactly the important point you can take away for yourself: Sometimes people who do us wrong make us understand the right thing, just in an incorrect way. If, after consulting with people and our own reflections, we realize that right is hidden in wrong, we should definitely have the ability to change.

Through the good coaxing of my friends, I gained the willingness to change. They helped me with the implementation. One good friend in particular knew a lot about fashion. My parents gave me money for 2 outfits; it was early pocket money. Now I also had the resources to transform. When I came to school the next day, the bullying gave way to speechless amazement and the first "human" tones I'd received. People developed interest in my transformation. What I needed was, in the end, banal: An environment that initially brought me enlightenment – albeit in an inappropriate way – consultation with my friends, plus a friend with fashion skills and finally styling as well as clothing as resources to put an end to the bullying.

All this does not say that my actions were correct. What made me realize that it was correct to "give in" to the mobbing crowd was how I felt afterwards. I felt more comfortable with the new style; the way I really was. I had turned my inner self inside out. Therefore, think carefully about whether the unjust harshness of others in your case does not have a justified core now and then.

If the money is there, it should sometimes be used to acquire resources, as long as they offer a realistic chance of achieving your personal goals. Your advantage in using resources to achieve goals is that they are there quickly: As soon as you make the consideration or payment, you have the resources you want.

Exercise 1

In your list, write down which resources, that will be available within a few days at the latest, can help you achieve your goals. Write down 5 resources for each goal, such as clothing for improved reputation, cars and/or bicycles for improved transportation, magazines and books for increased general knowledge or expertise, etc. After noting the resources that are plausible to you, check which ones are realistic in a timely manner and align with your beliefs. Anything that is not financially feasible for you, or that you feel would have little likelihood of helping you achieve your goal, you can safely cross off the list.

It gets more complex with the capabilities. Unlike resources, these are not available immediately. Here you are called upon to practice for a longer period of time and to work consistently. Some skills require more time and training to optimize, others less. If you are familiar with the respective skills because you have been practicing them for a long time, then you will be able to estimate well how much time and practice it will take you until the next increase. If you plan to learn new skills, be generous in estimating the time and practice required. Since you are not yet too familiar with the skill in question, you should leave yourself time cushions. To help you understand the message in this paragraph, here are 2 examples:

I.   You've been doing a job or hobby for several years. With that comes certain skills that you use every day – whether it's skills in programming software, fingers hovering over the piano, or your deft hand in drawing. You know these skills well and know what the next step is to increase. Consequently, you can estimate the time and practice required to successfully increase. These are familiar skills where you consequently plan very carefully.

II. You want to acquire a new skill that you have not practiced before. Perhaps the reason is that you have realized that what you have done so far is not for you. Now you want to do it all over again and are determined to succeed. Or you may want to acquire the ability to expand your existing skills. These and other scenarios confront you with the need to learn something completely new. Unlike a familiar skill, a new skill comes with more pitfalls because you have less knowledge about it and have a poor grasp of the processes required to improve it. For example, if you've never skated before, stumbling blocks could be that you buy the wrong equipment, lack talent and therefore need to practice more, and/or don't learn the technique optimally from the start, so all subsequent progress suffers. Therefore, be generous with the time you have available when learning new skills – rather a little more than too little.

Exercise 2

Now is the time for you, as a follow-up to Exercise 1 from this chapter and a continuation of your goals list from the previous chapters, identify the skills you could acquire to further your goals. The skills should always further your goals. Because you have formulated your goals in terms of your entire life – career, hobbies, family, etc. – having the appropriate skills ensures that you are furthering not only your professional life, but your life as a whole. Set priorities and time frames that fit your current situation. For example, if you have high ambitions in your career, it makes sense to develop new skills in this area first and only later devote yourself to skills that promote your hobbies.

Interim summary

Acquire resources and work on your skills to get closer to your desires and goals. In all of this, keep in mind that people who treat you unfairly can give you important clues to change. Sometimes it is beneficial to listen to people who are perceived to be unfair, as long as their incentives align with your own desires and goals.

3 tips to improve your skills

Training skills requires organization and regularity. Organization allows you to fit training into your daily routine and set the right priorities. Thanks to regularity you can always start at the level of the last training and build on it. In this way, you can follow the planned path step by step. The following 3 tips will help you with the 2 aspects of organization and regularity, but also make clear the importance of precise and patient practice.

Practice patiently and accurately from the beginning

This is a tip that comes first and to which many things should be subordinated. Learn 1 thing absolutely right from the beginning! What is meant by this? Don't be generous with technical or other types of errors in the 1st steps. Give mistakes the attention they deserve. Every mistake deserves absolute attention because it can negatively affect the other elements.

My experience

I often had this problem because I used to be impatient. Quick progress was more important to me than a solid foundation. That's how mistakes crept in later:

> When playing the piano, I always wanted to play fast and impress people with my speed. But since I never learned patiently at a slow tempo, especially the difficult passages of a piece became imprecise and unrhythmic.

> In weight training, I wanted to quickly increase my strength, which is why I only attached limited importance to technique. And so, it came to pass as it had to: when I was doing bench presses, my wrists were slightly over-bent, and when I did squats, my back was never absolutely straight. The result was regular injuries, after which I had to start again with lower weights.

> When I wrote my first book, I did it hastily and with the aim of publishing it as quickly as possible. The result was that it contained many spelling errors and colloquialisms. In addition, paragraphs devoid of content were the norm. I had to rewrite it completely.

This is real life. While on Instagram you have the ability to erase the mistakes from the piano piece or present a good excerpt from a weak book and charm people, none of that is feasible in real life. Keep that in mind, because some people are also blinded by the encouragement they receive on social media.

Ideally, you do things slowly and accurately from the start. That's exactly why it's also important to time your goals and skill training – so you have the opportunity to train slowly and patiently! All of the people who trained slower and more patiently than I did are much further along in their respective skills today.

Use 1-2-3 method

The 1-2-3 method is not only an aid for training your skills, but also for planning goals in general. In their book *Richtig priorisieren* (2014), the authors Proske et al. explain how tasks can be divided into 3 priority classes using this method.

➤ Prio 1 tasks
  ○ Main tasks with the highest priority, aligned with your most important objectives.
  ○ Should be scheduled regularly, tackled in good time (i.e., without time pressure), and addressed with high quality standards.
➤ Prio 2 tasks
  ○ Are not among your most important goals and are of secondary importance, but failure to complete them would still have negative consequences for you.
  ○ Should be specifically scheduled into the daily routine, possibly with the help of other people, and should be carried out with a much smaller amount of time (20:80 %) compared to the Prio 1 tasks.
➤ Prio 3 tasks
  ○ Unimportant tasks, which can possibly be postponed and whose non-completion would have no or only minor negative consequences for you.
  ○ Should not be worked through during the time of greatest concentration and should be completed as quickly as possible.

Source: Prioritize correctly (2014)

Create your own curriculum

The syllabus is used to visualize and record your plans in writing. You probably remember the lesson plans from school: 6 columns and several rows. In each row was a time slot in which you were taught a subject. In the columns of the top row, the days of the week Monday to Friday were entered, and in the rows below, in each column, the subjects matching the day and the respective time slot. You can now do the same for your skills training by writing down the 7 days of the week. Below that are the skills you want to train, and the time slots you want to schedule for it.

Time	Mo	Tue	Mi	Do	Fri	Sa	So
10-12 h							
12-14 h							
14-16 h							
...							

This table is only an approximate suggestion. Certainly, a time structure with time windows of less than 2 hours makes more sense. The advantage of such a plan is that you can plan and enter your whole life into it. If you make an individual schedule every week, you can even include variable activities, such as your wedding day or taking the kids to an event. This way you won't neglect any part of your life.

MPS Step 5 in brief

> ➢ Strengthening your own abilities provides a solid basis for your mental strength. Because the better you can do an activity, the less reason there is for negative emotions.

> ➢ You can also stop or mitigate external factors, such as bullying, by improving your skills – and sometimes even just by buying new resources, such as clothes. The important thing here is to only look to external factors as an impetus for change if you see a sense in them that appeals to you and aligns with your goals and desires.

> ➢ Training and improving your skills are also important in terms of human needs. You not only support your mental strength, but also work to a certain extent on your self-realization.

> ➢ Patience and accuracy are key when it comes to training. The more precisely you learn something, the less you have to touch it up afterwards.

> ➢ The 1-2-3 method, visualized lesson plans and daily schedules help you organize your training and keep it regular.

MPS Step 6: Keep going!

This book is designed to bring you change with its 5 steps. Change can take place in several directions. A positive direction is always desirable. You may think that the previous steps to mental strength can only lead you in a positive direction. But this is wrong: because the more you create and the stronger you become, the more realistic a significant side effect becomes: arrogance; arrogance, ignorance, gloating and other attitudes can become established in you the stronger and more superior you become. Please do not take this as a personal attack. The risk of arrogance is a factor that can affect all people.

My experience

I, too, have already had the opportunity to experience what it is like to become arrogant. As announced in the introduction, my path to mental strength played out exactly as in this book: First, I acquired mental strength roughly on the basis of the first 5 steps. Then I was happy and strong. Unfortunately, I became arrogant. I mocked people who did not achieve individual goals. Moreover, I only respected the strong person who was able to overcome his emotions. Nothing could stop my arrogance. People stuck by me despite my character; possibly because they still saw the former good in me. Only when I was confronted with a power that was new and unattainable to me did my thinking change. This power was health. I suffered an illness that, frankly, wasn't that bad. But it was troublesome, and the doctors didn't know what it was. In part, it made me frantic. As I lay in bed at night or sat on my sofa,

I thought. I decided to change things. Eventually, my illness – or rather, the ominous complaint – was gone again. I had learned from that phase. There is always a way down again...

To make this downward path as unlikely as possible for you, it is important that you remain down to earth. Sharing successes with other people, working together and living together peacefully is important balm for the soul. This chapter will give you some theories and lessons to keep in mind, especially as your success increases, to always understand that strength and success are not a permanent gift but are fleeting. This is the last important lesson in mental strength: to be able to deal with the newfound success.

Lesson 1: Be kind and respectful to your enemies

What is an enemy anyway? Every person has his or her own opinion because it is largely a question of one's own attitude. While some see a person as an enemy who constantly says negative things about them behind their back, others see this as something that is normal in life. Because there will always be people who are not well-disposed towards you.

This first lesson is about such enemies: As long as a person does not take active steps against you that endanger your professional life, family or health, there is no reason to consider them a serious enemy. Most of the time, they are people who have problems in their own lives or are weak and are trying to mask that so they go on the attack. Especially with increasing mental strength and increasing success in the various areas of your life, you will encounter people who are not well-disposed towards you. As long as they do not harm you in an acutely dangerous way but limit their actions to negative talk and small pranks, it is best to position yourself as well-disposed towards these people. This way you have a chance to change your enemies. For these persons, who may have experienced little kindness in their lives, could be moved to rethink by your well-meaning behavior.

It is important to position yourself respectfully and sympathetically towards your enemy, especially in order not to get into the line of fire through bad luck. What if your opponent's hostility at work went unnoticed, but your counterattacks did not? Then you would risk warnings and a deteriorated reputation. Moreover, a hostile attitude may have a negative effect on your subconscious: You feel bad deep down because you are lowering yourself to the level of your enemy. This negatively affects your actions and creates a psychological burden.

Do not be reserved and do not make yourself a victim, but refrain from unnecessary actions and words against your enemies. You have the mental strength for this thanks to the learned impulse control and the principle of the present.

Lesson 2: Never forget where you came from

Where you come from – this means your former (more difficult) situation without mental strength. Before this book and its activities, teachings, and experiences, you were in a different situation than you are now. There is hope that you have become stronger. Strength leads to new possibilities and perspectives. If you take advantage of these, then your success is most likely to increase. With this comes a danger: You could take off.

Success has the ability to dazzle. This ability does not come from success itself, but from deep within you. If you do not regularly put yourself back in the position you were in before, it is quite possible that you will become arrogant over time. Therefore, practice humility and accept that you can do some things and not others at the same time. Remember that there are still some things about you that you can work on. And above all, *remember that there will always be things that you cannot change*. Always see your abilities as needing improvement and recognize your limitations. Then you will move closer to humility and modesty, which is essential for you to stay grounded and not take off. Also, avoid judging others because they have their own problems and challenges to deal with. Think back to yourself and realize that basically any person can become successful. Build up the people around you rather than putting them down – this way you won't be confronted with your own past and the hard road to success.

Lesson 3: Give and take are both necessary

What is wealth worth if it is only stashed away? Whether you are *successful*, rich in money or rich in love, wealth that is not used has little or no value. Let's imagine that you are a person with strong social skills, and you also have all the qualities for a committed relationship or marriage. You are faithful, have plenty of time, remember wedding anniversaries and birthdays, love children. You are rich in love. But you lock yourself up at home because you have suffered a loss, or you are afraid of not experiencing the same love from other people. Dramatic is such a scenario where you are rich in love but do not share that love. The same goes for money, success and other components of life: if you don't share, it's hard for you to enjoy it. This leads to the realization that you should spend money now and then – wisely, of course – if you want to feel your wealth. You should show love to others in order to experience it. Success is inspiring for yourself, but only under the encouragement and appreciation of others do you realize how successful you really are.

Life is a give and take. You give something – even something immaterial, such as your affection or your understanding – and receive something else in return. So, giving doesn't necessarily have to take place on a material level, but can also be intangible. You have several chances to give people what they need. Listen to people's wants and needs and give what seems possible and appropriate to you. Approach people with your "riches" and let them share. This is the best way to establish a position from which people will be grateful and well-disposed toward you.

Lesson 4: Use power to achieve goals with others

When you achieve mental strength, you also gain the competence to lead other people. "Leading" is a broad concept: On the one hand, you can advance professionally and become a department head or managing director. On the other hand, it is conceivable that you do not achieve any particular goals professionally, but instead build up an environment with people who perceive you as a leader. A leader is not necessarily characterized by a professional position or a special career. Nor does he have to have achieved a great deal in his private life. What distinguishes a leader is his charisma. This charisma is based on the fact that you have faith in yourself and in your plans. It gives you unassailability, which makes an impression on other people.

Charisma is an important keyword here. If you leave people with an aura of mental strength, you have the chance to achieve goals together with them. They will gladly follow you if your goals coincide with theirs. This gives you the opportunity to deepen relationships with those around you and move forward faster. Together you reach your goals faster.

Example

You have a fascinating idea for a business and start a company. Over time, you want it to grow. In the 1st case, you find it difficult to part with tasks and delegate them to other people. Because you do everything on your own, you don't have time to take care of the growth of your business. In the 2nd case, you enlist the help of other people and manage them wisely as a leader, giving them the opportunity to contribute their own ideas and merge them with yours. After you have made the final decision, people are happy to put your wishes into practice because they are allowed to act independently, and you do not interfere with them. In this case, nothing stands in the way of your company's growth.

Closing words

Developing and expanding mental strength is beneficial for any person in any situation in life. Especially MPS Step 6 has shown that mental strength is not only about having it. It is equally necessary to be able to handle it. Otherwise, there is the threat of arrogance, and with time, as a logical consequence, the loss of what you have worked for. Therefore, this book is a perfect permanent reading in life. Read it regularly – perhaps every year, every 2 years, or every 5 years. There will always be things, with time, that you can still work on with the help of the steps and teachings in this book.

I have read many books and had many experiences on my way to a mentally stronger personality. In the process, I have made use of 1 thing that, unfortunately, no author has directly recommended: I read each book several times and still do. Why? Quite simply: because I want to avoid *experiencing* bad things and because I want to learn them or remember them again. Therefore, it is best to handle it the same way. My father was once in Thailand and told me about his trip. I remembered 1 thing in particular. I don't know why, but the story of his visit to a temple left a lasting impression on me. Perhaps a part of me knew even then that they would be important words for my life. He told me that it was the custom there to kneel down and say several times in one's mind what one would like to become or do. One should tell oneself what should become better. Several hundred times one should do it regularly to remember it later.

What my father told me and what I did with the repeated reading of several books is another difference between mentally strong and mentally weak people: the ability to learn through narratives, affirmations, and from the lives of others. You have a choice to learn from the mistakes of others or from your own. It lends itself better to learning from the mistakes of others. So read this and other helpful books several times to internalize and remember the content. Listen to other people when they tell you things and warn you. Think about whether it might be better to rein yourself in. This will reduce the likelihood of gross mistakes on your part in the long run and maintain the mental strength you have gained with the help of this book.

Work constantly to deepen and retain what you have gained with the help of this guidebook. Because mental strength is like many other things in life: building it up is difficult and tedious work. Losing it can often happen in a very short time. All it takes is 1 wrong decision in which you violate the principles you have learned. Or you set 1 goal too many, which throws your objectives and priorities into chaos.

Therefore, cherish your mental strength and do everything you can to preserve it!

References

Heller, J.: *Resilienz – 7 Schlüssel für mehr innere Stärke.* München: Gräfe und Unzer Verlag GmbH, 2013.

Janson, M.: *Resilienz trainieren – Wie Sie innere Blockaden lösen, Ihre psychische Widerstandskraft stärken und stressfrei alle Krisen überstehen!.* 2020.

Lorenz, S.: *Resilienz entwickeln: „Ich schaffe das!" – Wie du deine innere Stärke entfaltest, um an Stress, Krisen und Schicksalsschlägen nicht zu zerbrechen.* 2020.

Moestl, B.: *Shaolin – Du musst nicht kämpfen, um zu siegen.* München: Droemer Knaur. 2008.

Proske, H.: Reichert, J. F.; Reiff, E.: *Richtig priorisieren.* Freiburg: Haufe-Lexware GmbH & Co. KG, 2014.

Späth, Dr. T.; Bao, S. Y.: *Shaolin – Das Geheimnis der inneren Stärke.* München: Gräfe und UNZER Verlag GmbH, 2011.

Stangl, W.: Online Lexikon für Psychologie und Pädagogik, 2020.

Webb, R.; Pedersen, C.; Mok, P.: *Adverse Outcomes to Early Middle Age Linked With Childhood Residential Mobility.* American Journal of Preventive Medicine, 2016.

Printed in Great Britain
by Amazon

27421095R00069